In a Manner of Speaking

To John.

Best wishes

Charlie Hoy

16·05·17

In a Manner of Speaking

The Story of the English Language

CHARLIE HAYLOCK & BARRIE APPLEBY

AMBERLEY

To Ruth

First published 2017

Amberley Publishing
The Hill, Stroud
Gloucestershire, GL5 4EP

www.amberley-books.com

British Library Cataloguing in Publication Data.
A catalogue record for this book is available from the British Library.

ISBN 978 1 4456 6382 1 (paperback)
ISBN 978 1 4456 6383 8 (ebook)

Typesetting and Origination by Amberley Publishing.
Printed in the UK.

Contents

Introduction

Why do we have so many dialects in England?

Why do we not all speak in standard English?

Why do we pronounce differently some words which are spelled the same?

Why are there ten different pronunciations of *ough*?

Why do we say *lefftenant*, when it's spelled 'lieutenant'?

Why is English grammatically the easiest European language, and yet the most difficult for its various spellings and pronunciations?

In a Manner of Speaking will answer these questions and more.

Each chapter will show, in a chronological order, the evolution of spoken English; how each invading force brought their different sounds; how history has influenced the English language and how the English tongue has evolved through time.

This book does not concentrate on English grammar ... it is mainly about the evolution of how English is spoken, even in its birthplace, England ... and why we have so many variations.

It has been written in an easy-to-read style, interspersed with humour in the superb illustrations by the renowned cartoonist Barrie Appleby.

In a Manner of Speaking has evolved from my lectures on the history of spoken English. Mainly these talks were in East Anglia, but due to increasing demand I have ventured much further afield and also, by popular request, I have responded by writing a book on this intriguing subject.

I hope you enjoy reading *In a Manner of Speaking* as much as I did writing it.

Charlie Haylock

Maria Legg at an Anglo-Saxon re-enactment

Maria was the voice of *Æðelflæd, Lady of the Mercians* for Michael Wood's BBC production, *King Alfred and the Anglo Saxons* and also the many female voices in the audio accompaniment to Matt Love's book, *Learn Old English with Leofwin*.

Foreword

The history of the English language is a complex and fascinating one, the subject matter endlessly shifting and adapting in step with the broader history of the people who speak it. Indeed, a history of the language must necessarily be a history of its people too.

In a Manner of Speaking takes the reader on a journey of discovery from the origins of Old English in northern Europe to the abbreviated language of texts used today. Along the way we meet many familiar names such as Chaucer and Shakespeare but also a host of new characters who all have their part to play in this great story.

This book therefore is a history of English-speaking people, complete with all the relevant events both large and small which have helped to shape the language we speak today. Invasions and expansions, cricket and cocktails – Charlie Haylock has captured them all in this enjoyable and informative book, clearly presented in chronological order together with the wonderful illustrations of Barrie Appleby.

But this is not just a book about language and history. This is *our* story.

Maria Legg, independent scholar

Acknowledgements

After a lifetime study, to write an abridged summary of history and how it has influenced spoken English, without getting bogged down with too much detail, was indeed a mammoth task. *In a Manner of Speaking* is an easy-to-read overview of how English has progressed chronologically from the Celts to the present day. Barrie Appleby's cartoons and drawings help make it an enjoyable read. However, if *In a Manner of Speaking* whets the appetite of the reader for further learning and a greater depth of knowledge in any particular area – and hopefully it will – then the following authors and publications, to which I am indebted, are highly recommended.

David Crystal is a living legend on the English language, both spoken and written, and his *The Stories of English* delves deeper into the history of English and is much more detailed. For further reading into Shakespearian English then David and Ben Crystal's *Oxford Illustrated Shakespeare Dictionary* will cover every aspect in an entertaining way.

The Adventure of English by Melvyn Bragg and *The Story of English* by Robert McCrum, William Cran and Robert MacNeil are excellent longer publications, again digging deeper into the subject.

To delve into the wonderful intricacies of the origins and meanings of English surnames and place names, then books and dictionaries by P. H. Reaney and A. D. Mills respectively are absolute treasures.

When God Spoke English by Adam Nicolson focuses on the fascinating history that surrounds the King James Bible. Details of these and other publications are listed in the Bibliography.

I must thank Barrie Appleby for his wonderful, funny and telling cartoons, which highlight many aspects of *In a Manner of Speaking* in a humorous fashion. And a big thank you to Jason Appleby of Ark Design, Sudbury, for his help in formatting the illustrations; Maria and 'Wobbly' Legg for supplying accurate re-enactment photos; and to David Mills, Emeritus Reader in Medieval English, University of London, for guidance and informal consultations.

Last but not least, one big thank you must go to Ruth Gitsham, Librarian at The Royal Hospital School, Holbrook, Suffolk. Without her, this book would have taken a lot longer to complete. Ruth's proofreading and help with research, compiling and collating was immensely helpful and greatly appreciated, and why 'To Ruth' is on the title verso page.

1

Celtic Britons

The Ancient Celts were a collection of tribes who occupied a great expanse of modern-day Europe. Their territories stretched from the British and Irish shores in the north-west, way down to France and the Iberian Peninsula in the south-west and in a wide band across to and including eastern Europe.

Civilisations and expanding empires from other regions, including the Romans, decimated the various Celtic tribes. This takeover was achieved slowly but often with great violence, either by enslavement or a complete destruction of their Celtic cultures. The surviving Celts were gradually pushed over to the edge of the western shores of Europe.

The remaining undisputed Celtic strongholds today are Wales (*Cymru*), Cornwall (*Kernow*), Brittany (*Breizh*), the Isle of Man (*Mannin Ellan Vannin*), Scotland (*Alba*) and Ireland (*Eire*). They each have their own indigenous Celtic language that is still being spoken by a good number of the population in the twenty-first century; namely, *Cymraeg* (Welsh), *Kernowek* (Cornish), *Brezhoneg* (Breton), *Gaelg* (Manx), *Gaidhlig* (Scottish Gaelic) and *Gaeilge* (Irish).

Scottish Gaelic, Manx and Irish are tightly interlinked Gaelic Celtic languages, whilst Welsh, Cornish and Breton belong to the southern Brythonic group. The former are very similar in sound and structure; so much so that there are many examples of Irish and Manx speakers conversing with their Scottish counterparts in their various Gaelic tongues and being readily understood by one another. The same can be said about the Welsh and Cornish speakers being able to converse with Bretons from northern France in their own distinctive Brythonic dialects.

Historians are divided as to whether the Basque area of Spain and south-west France is of Celtic origin. It would appear that the argument for and against is equally balanced and this will therefore remain a talking point with no definite conclusion.

The Ancient Celtic Britons were a collection of tribes whose names were thankfully recorded by the Romans, who Latinised what they found. Historians throughout the ages have used these Latinised Celtic names ever since, from the *Cantiaci* in modern-day Kent, the *Brigantes* in the Lake District, the *Dumnonii* in the far south-west, the *Iceni* in East Anglia and numerous tribes everywhere in between.

The Brythonic, or Brittonic, language that the Ancient Britons spoke is very similar to modern Welsh and Cornish.

There are a number of examples where the Brythonic language still survives today in the English language. Many English place names have Celtic origins, sometimes with humorous outcomes. Breedon on the Hill is a prime example: *Bre* was the name given to several ancient British settlements on a hill, and so called because *bre* is Brythonic for 'hill'. When the Anglo-Saxons arrived they adopted some of the place names called Bre, and because they were on a hill, they renamed some as *Breodun*. The suffix *-dun* is Old English (Anglo-Saxon) for 'hill'. It transpired that eventually there was more than one place called Breedon, so in the Middle Ages, to distinguish one Breedon from another, one was called Breedon on the Hill, which translates from its different linguistic origins as 'hill, hill on the hill'.

A great number of English river names have Brythonic roots, too, with similar consequences. The River Avon is a very good example. *Afon* or *avon* is Brythonic for 'river', as it is in the Welsh language today. Once again, the Anglo-Saxons adopted the name and called it the River Avon, which translates back as 'river river'.

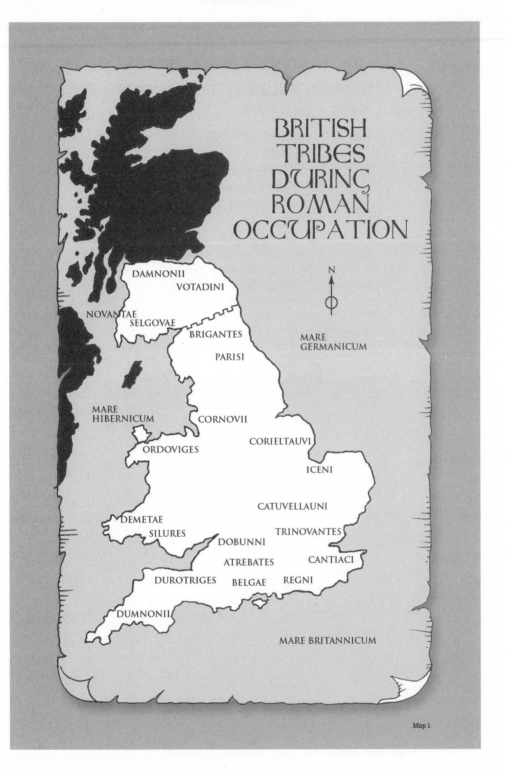

BRITISH
TRIBES
DURING
ROMAN
OCCUPATION

N

DAMNONII
VOTADINI
NOVANTAE
SELGOVAE
BRIGANTES
PARISI
MARE
GERMANICUM
MARE
HIBERNICUM
CORNOVII
ORDOVIGES
CORIELTAUVI
ICENI
CATUVELLAUNI
DEMETAE
SILURES
TRINOVANTES
DOBUNNI
ATREBATES
CANTIACI
DUROTRIGES
BELGAE
REGNI
DUMNONII
MARE BRITANNICUM

Map 1

Some English place names & rivers with Brythonic roots

Brythonic word	meaning	places and rivers
ardu	high	Forest of Arden
afon	river	River Avon
bre	hill	Bredon, Brewood, Breedon-on-the-Hill, Brill
briga	hill	Brent, Brentford, Bryn
crug	hill	Creech St Michael, Crewkerne, Crich, Crickheath, Cricklade
dubr	water	Dover
eburo	yew	York
iska	water	River Axe, Axminster, Axmouth, River Esk, Eskeleth, River Exe, Exebridge, Exford, Exeter, Exminster, Exton
pen	hill top	Pencoyd, Pencraig, Pendlebury, Pendock, Penge, Pengethley, Penketh, Penn, Penrith, Penshaw
tames	dark	River Tamar, River Tame x 3, River Team, River Thames

Note - Cornwall has a very high percentage of Brythonic place names beginning with pen, pol, porth, tre and many more, showing their Brythonic roots.

Fig 1

2

The Romans

The Romans invaded Britain and became an occupying force for nearly 400 eventful years. Yet, believe it or not, they had very little influence on the creation or evolution of the English language. But indirectly they did.

The first couple of fairly unsuccessful Roman invasions were led by Julius Caesar in 55 BC and 54 BC. It was not until AD 43, some one hundred years later during the time of Emperor Claudius, that General Aulus Plautius led the most effective invasion with long-term consequences – so much so that Plautius was installed as the first Roman governor of Britain.

The Roman governors and administrators Latinised the names of the British towns and villages they encountered, such as the ancient village of Mam, which was Latinised to *Mamucium, then Mancunium*, later to be known as Manchester. Likewise, *Londinium* derives from the Celtic British for a river crossing and it was eventually anglicised to London.

The Romans also built settlements and fortifications in new locations and gave them Latin names, which were invariably anglicised at a later date. *Ad Pontes* ('the bridges') became known as Staines, which is Old English (Anglo-Saxon) for stones. *Caesaromago*, meaning 'market of Caesar', was later called Chelmsford, which translates as the ford belonging to an Anglo-Saxon called Ceolmaer. The Roman spa, *Aquae Sulis* ('waters of the Roman goddess *Sulis*') is known today as Bath, from the Old English *baeth*.

Although the Roman ruling classes, administrators, scribes, teachers and cartographers wrote their manuscripts in Latin, they spoke to each other mainly in Ancient Greek. The Romans had studied Greek history and based their own rule and the building of an empire on

Grecian lines. They tried to copy them in every way and even tried to adopt their language. However, the Roman soldiers came from all four corners of the Empire and did not speak learned Latin or Greek. They spoke the language from whence they came. The Ancient Britons would have heard a multitude of exotic foreign languages because the Roman Empire stretched across Europe, from Britain and parts of present-day Germany down into Africa, including the countries on the shores of the Mediterranean, and through to the Middle East. It was soon realised that the troops from these much warmer climates were finding it very difficult to work efficiently in the unfavourable conditions of the inclement British weather.

Therefore, the Romans drafted a good number of their occupying troops from the northern end of their empire, and also employed mercenaries from these Germanic tribes as well. Many of the troops brought their families over to Britain and settled, creating several Germanic-speaking settlements within Roman-controlled Celtic Britain. The seeds of a future Germanic tongue were being sown.

During the Roman occupation, the south coast of present-day Lincolnshire and that of East Anglia, Essex and Kent was given the name *Litus Saxonicum,* translated as the 'Saxon Shore'. A number of strategic fortifications were built along this vulnerable coastline, arguably to protect it from any threat of invasion from the Northern European Germanic tribes outside the Roman Empire. Ironically, though, this threat did not seem to include the Saxons, and yet the Romans named it *Litus Saxonicum*; the kind of misconception that has happened throughout history.

The creation of the Saxon Shore meant that trading routes were also established with northern Europe, even with tribes that were outside the northern limits of the Roman Empire. The Britons were now meeting and interacting with many people speaking a Germanic tongue on a daily basis, either from the Roman occupying forces or through the traders on the shore.

During this long association with the Romans the various Germanic tribes, whilst negotiating or in conversation, adopted the Latin word *castra*, meaning 'a Roman settlement'. Later, the Anglo-Saxons' vernacular version became *ceaster,* and their own dialectal variations provided different pronunciations for *chester, caster, caister, cester,* etc. The Anglo-Saxons, not the Romans, created these English place names.

In AD 388 the Romans started to leave Britain, and by AD 410 the last of the occupying forces departed to try and defend Rome. They left

behind a people mainly speaking a British Celtic tongue. Only the British ruling elite in the south and east were able to converse in what is called British Latin or British Vulgar Latin. Some of the Germanic troops and their families stayed behind in a few well-established settlements. It has recently been suggested that Ingham in Suffolk derives its name from the homestead settlement (*ham*) belonging to the leader of a Germanic tribe called the *Inguiones*. They were mentioned by Tacitus, a Roman historian (AD 56–c. 117). It's believed that the *Inguiones* remained in their village-type encampment after the Romans had left. This settlement would have included Britons as well as the *Inguiones*.

It is reasonable to assume that throughout Britain there were other places similar to Ingham having a Germanic connection well before the arrival of the Angles and Saxons. It is also reasonable to assume that some would have intermarried and that the Britons were now very used to hearing Germanic-speaking people. A few more seeds of a Germanic tongue were being sown.

By the end of the Roman occupation the Britons and the Romans had been converted to Christianity. It was really now for the first time that the majority of Britons were hearing Latin being spoken on a regular basis via the clergy and the Church. This Latin influence was to be short-lived and had very little effect, if any at all, on the evolution of the English language as we know it today. Only a few Latin words at this time in history had been permanently adopted by the Britons. However, it would have a bigger impact later on under the West Saxon ruler, Alfred the Great.

The reason why it was so evanescent is that the Romans left for good in AD 410 and the Christian British culture was in for a shock. The pagan Germanic tribes of northern Europe were about to arrive in force. These various groups, known collectively as the 'English', would settle and dominate. This supremacy was achieved over a comparatively short period of time.

The Roman occupation had lasted for nearly four hundred years from AD 43 to 410. They greatly influenced the infrastructure of Britain at the time, and there are still many remnants of that occupation in the present day. Several towns are built on old Roman sites and some of our roadways follow the lines of those constructed by the Romans. The names of most of the British tribes at the time are known today only by the names the Romans gave them, otherwise they would be anonymous or forgotten.

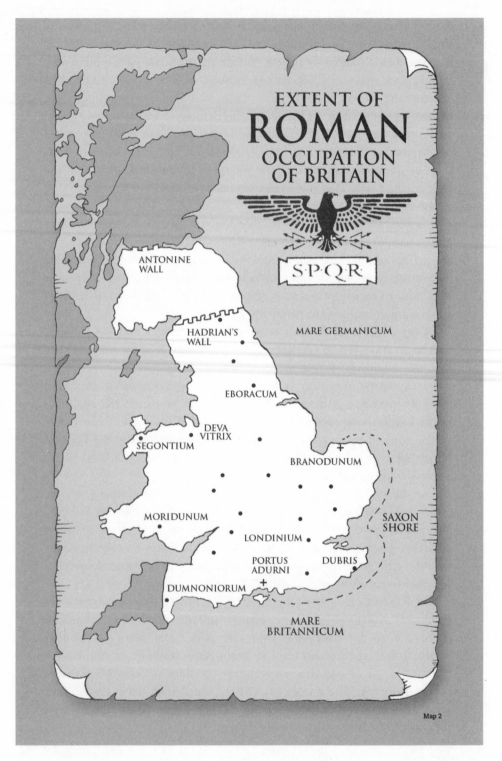

EXTENT OF
ROMAN
OCCUPATION
OF BRITAIN

S·P·Q·R

ANTONINE WALL

HADRIAN'S WALL

MARE GERMANICUM

EBORACUM

DEVA VITRIX

SEGONTIUM

BRANODUNUM

MORIDUNUM

SAXON SHORE

LONDINIUM

PORTUS ADURNI

DUBRIS

DUMNONIORUM

MARE BRITANNICUM

Map 2

English Place Name today	Roman Name	OE Name 1086AD	OE (Old English) Meaning 'Old Roman fort that is . . .'
Acaster	Valcaester	Aecaster	by adopted Celtic river name
Alcester	Alauna	Alencester	by adopted Celtic river name
Ancaster	unknown	Anecaster	occupied by A-S called Anna
Bicester	unknown	Bernecester	occupied by by A-S warriors
Binchester	Vinovia	Vincaester	unknown
Brancaster	Branodunum	Broncester	Anglicised Celtic - 'crow fort'
Caistor	Castrum	Caster	old Roman fort
Caistor St Edmund	Casrtum	Caster	dedicated to St Edmund
Caister-on-Sea	Castrum	Caster	'on-Sea' added much later
Casterton	unknown	Caestertun	by a farmstead settlement
Castor	Durobrivae?	Caester	old Roman fort
Chester	Deva Vitrix	Caester	old Roman fort
Chesterfield	unknown	Cesterfelda	next to open cultivated land
Chesterford	unknown	Caesterforda	at a shallow river crossing
Chester-le-Street	Concangis	Caesterstraet	by a Roman road
Chesterton (Cambs, Oxon, Staffs, War)	-	Caestertun (or similar)	by a farmstead settlement
Chesterwood	unknown	Caesterwode	by the wood
Chichester	Noviomagus Reginorum	Cissecaester	occupied by A-S called Cisse
Cirencester	Corinium	Cirencaester	Anglicised Celtic name
Colchester	Camulodunum	Colnecaester	by the River Colne
Doncaster	Danum	Donecaester	by the River Don
Dorchester, (Dor)	Durnovaria	Dorecester	Anglicised Celtic name
Dorchester -on-Thames	Dorcic	Dorchecester	Anglicised Celtic name
Ebchester	Vindomora	Ebbescester	occupied by A-S called Ebbes
Exeter	Isca Dumnoniorum	Execester	by adopted Celtic river name
Frocester	unknown	Frowecester	by adopted Celtic river name
Gloucester	Glevum	Glowecester	in a bright place
Godmanchester	Durovigutum	Godmundcester	occupied by A-S Godmund

Grantchester is not a *caester* - derives from Granteseta - OE for settlers (*setta*) on the River Granta

Fig 2

English Place Name today	Roman Name	OE Name 1086AD	OE (Old English) Meaning 'Old Roman fort that is ...'
Hincaster	unknown	Hennecaster	haunted by wild birds
Ilchester	Lindinis	Givelcester (pron Yiuelchester)	by River Gifl (pron yiwle) adopted Celtic river name
Irchester	unknown	Irencester	occupied by A-S called Yra
Kenchester	unknown	Chenecester	occupied by A-S called Cena
Lancaster	Lanecastrum	Loncaster	adopted Celtic river name
Lanchester	Longovicium	Langecester	a long fortification
Leicester	Ratae Corieltauvorum	Ligeracester	occupied by A-S Ligore
Mancetter	Manduessedum	Manacaster	unknown
Manchester	Mancunium	Mamecester	Anglicised Celtic for a hill, either, shaped like a breast or dedicated to a mother god
Muncaster	unknown	Muncaester	poss OE *mund* for protector
Portchester	Portus Adurni	Portecaester	by the harbour
Ribchester	Bremetennacum	Ribelcaster	by the River Ribble
Rocester	unknown	Rowcester	rough earthworks
Rochester, Kent	Durobrivae	Rovecester	by the bridges
Rochester, Northum	Bremennium	Ruhcaester	rough earthworks
Silchester	Calleva Atrebatum	Sielecaester	by the willow copse
Tadcaster	Calcaria	Tatecaster	occupied by A-S called Tata
Towcester	Lactodorum	Tovecester	by the River Tove

Uttoxeter is not a *caester* - derives from Wotocheshede - OE for *haeddre* (heath) owned by **Wottoc**

Winchester	Venta Belgarum	Wincester	adopted Celtic name
Worcester	Vertis?	Wirecester	adopted Celtic river name
Wroxeter	Viroconium Cornoviorum	Rochecester	adopted Celtic name poss from Wreocen, Wrekin

Note; In Anglo-Saxon times, *caester* had a variety of spellings with different pronunciations. This eventually led to the variations of the present day, including caister, caistor, caster, castor, cester, cetter, chester and main component of xeter.

1086AD is the date of the Domesday Book

Fig 2 II

There are several other examples of the Roman legacy, but they had very little direct influence, if any, on the future of the English language. But indirectly they did. For instance, the Romans employed Germanic troops and mercenaries as their occupying force, some of whom, along with their families, continued to live in Britain after the Roman occupation had ended.

The four hundred years of Roman occupation had affected the Celtic Britons' way of life and split the nation in two. The military and social control of the Romans was seen as beneficial by the British chieftains in the south-east of the country, but quite the opposite by the tribal leaders from the north and west. However, for the vast majority of the time the enforced occupation had little or no effect on ordinary folk. The Ancient Britons were mainly peasants and as such were tied to the soil well before the Romans came, and remained so.

To reward certain people, such as officials and high-ranking soldiers within their service, the Romans granted Roman citizenship. It was a way of recognising those loyal to Rome and meant they enjoyed the privileges exclusive to being a citizen of the empire. This procedure was also used by the Romans to try and get the Celtic British kings and nobility onside. They would however, have to swear allegiance to Rome, and although several tribal kings and chieftains did so, a good number did not. The overall effect was to split the Celtic Britons in half. The tribal lords who continued to be beholden to their ancient ways and customs were not favoured by the Romans and were not granted citizenship. However, an ordinary peasant carried on as normal whether citizenship had been granted or not.

The British kings and nobility that did 'sign up' to Roman citizenship would most probably have learned some form of Latin, both spoken and written. This version of Latin is recognised as Vernacular Latin, which can best be described as Vulgar Latin with a Brythonic dialect. As a result, a few Latin words were adopted by the British into their Brythonic vocabulary.

When the Romans departed for good, they left behind a divided British people who were split into two main factions: those who wanted to revert back to the old Celtic ways and those who wanted a structured society and the law and order of the Romans. Subsequently, there ensued internal strife and fighting that culminated in what might loosely be described as a civil war.

Britain was now very vulnerable and ready for the taking, and the Germanic tribes from northern Europe were getting ready to take their chance. The English tribes were on their way.

THE FIRST INVASION OF THE GERMANIC TRIBES

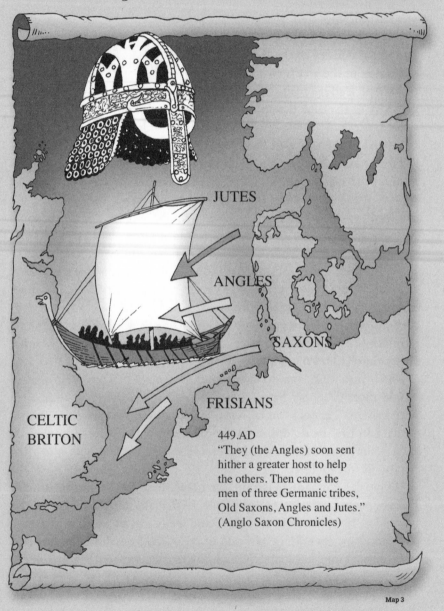

JUTES

ANGLES

SAXONS

FRISIANS

CELTIC BRITON

449.AD
"They (the Angles) soon sent hither a greater host to help the others. Then came the men of three Germanic tribes, Old Saxons, Angles and Jutes."
(Anglo Saxon Chronicles)

Map 3

3

The English

Who are the English and where did they come from?

'The English' is a collective name retrospectively given to the various Germanic tribes from Northern Europe who came marauding, pillaging and ravaging the British shores in the fifth, sixth and seventh centuries, eventually settling on the island. They were principally a haphazard mix of Angles (from where the term 'English' derives), Saxons, Jutes and Frisians, who all spoke the same Germanic language but with different dialects. Back in their homelands, these Germanic dialects have grown apart and become separate languages, albeit closely linked, but in England they merged together to lay the foundation for the English language.

The Angles, or *Engelisc*, pronounced *Engelish*, came from Angeln just south of the current Danish/German border. Some historians have suggested that Angeln is located in that area of north-western Europe which was inhabited by Vikings, and that the Angles were in fact the southern faction of the Scandinavian people. It is believed that the *Wuffingas*, the ruling hierarchy of the East Angles, who had links with the Swedish royal dynasty, occupied the same part of Jutland as the Angles. Later in time, they arrived on the east coast and became the kings of the East Angles, settling in present-day Cambridgeshire, Norfolk and Suffolk. There are strong grounds for this school of thought. Firstly, the Angle weaponry, armoury and other artefacts found in East Anglia, such as those at the internationally important Angle burial ship in Sutton Hoo, Suffolk, are exactly the same in design and pattern as the Viking discoveries around Uppsala, in southern Sweden. Excavations in other parts of England have uncovered finds from the fifth and sixth centuries which, although very similar, are always slightly different, suggesting they had influences from somewhere other than just the southern Swedes via the Angles and Angeln.

Secondly, one of the most important pieces of early English literature, if not the most important, is the oldest surviving written document of the ancient epic poem *Beowulf*. This heroic saga is another sizeable piece of evidence to endorse the south Swedish link with the Angles. Originally handed down by word of mouth, it is of Scandinavian origin incorporating the Angles, Jutes and Frisians. It was adopted and adapted by the Angles and later by the Saxons. Eventually, after hundreds of years, it was written down anonymously in the eleventh century in English.

There is some discussion as to the derivation of the name *Angeln*. Some scholars say it derives from the word *anglen*, which described the shape of the land where some of the Angles inhabited. A piece of land jutted out from the mainland and it was likened to the shape of a hook; in other words, an angle (Old English *angel,* pronounced 'angle'). This is also why fishermen today who use a hook (angle) on the end of a line are called anglers. Incidentally, the Old English word *angeltwicce,* literally translated as 'angle twitch', was the name given to the wriggling worm on the hook used as fishing bait. Another hypothesis is that it derives from the root word *ange* or *enge*, which also describes the area, being a narrow strip of land. I tend to favour the fish hook theory as it holds more water and is much more feasible.

The Jutes came from Jutland, which is now primarily mainland Denmark and part of Scandinavia, just north of where the Angles originated. Some historians have also categorised the Jutes as being Viking because of their original Scandinavian location.

The Saxons came from the present-day Schleswig-Holstein area of north-west Germany, just south of the Angles. They were so called because of the short sword they used in close-combat fighting, which was known as a *seax*. A longsword or two-handed sword was too unwieldy and cumbersome, ineffective at close quarters; but the *seax* was a lethal and very efficient fighting weapon in the right hands. The warriors with the short swords were therefore known as the *Seaxan*.

Although the Germanic Saxons spoke a language similar to the Angles and Jutes, called West Germanic, they are not considered to be part of the Old Scandinavian or Old Norse sub-sections of Germanic languages.

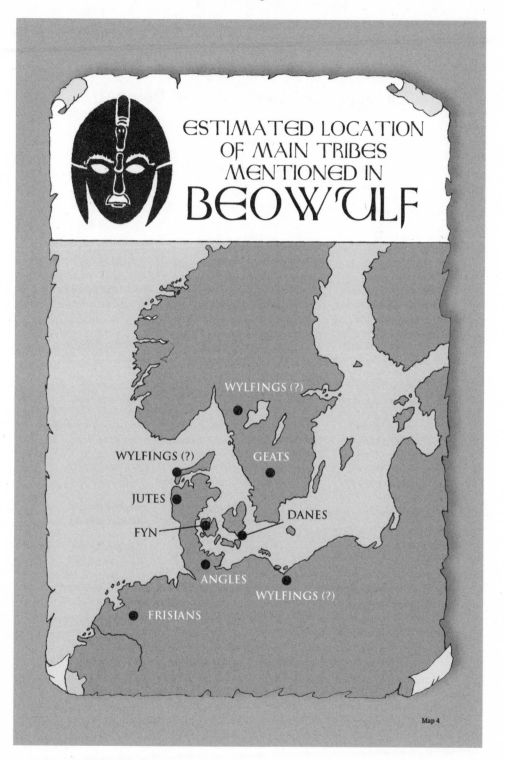

ESTIMATED LOCATION
OF MAIN TRIBES
MENTIONED IN
BEOWULF

WYLFINGS (?)

WYLFINGS (?)

GEATS

JUTES

FYN

DANES

ANGLES

WYLFINGS (?)

FRISIANS

Map 4

Excerpt from beginning of Béowulf

Hwæt What (listen)!	*Wé Gár-Denain* We the Spear Danes	*géardagum* in days gone by
þéodcyninga and the kings	*þrym gefrúnon* who ruled them with glory	*hú ðá æþelinguas* and how those princes
ellen fremedon bravely fought.	*Oft Scyld Scéfing* Often, Scyld Scéfing	*sceaþena þréatum* scourged the enemy
monegum mǽgþum from many peoples	*meodosetla oftéah* and took away mead benches and	*egsode eorlas* terrorised earls,
syððan ǽrest wearð after first himself being held to ransom	*féasceaft funden* and found destitute	*hé þæs frófre gebád* he would later prosper.
wéox under wolcnum He grew under the heavens	*weorðmyndum þáh* with worthiness therein	*oðþæt him ǽghwyle* until everyone to him
þǽra ittendra from the surrounding tribes	*ofer hronráde* beyond the whale road	*hýran scolde* was submissive,
gomban gyldan and paid tribute.	*þæt wæs gód cyning* That was being a good king.	*Ðǽm eafera wæs* To him an heir
æfter cenned afterwards was born,	*geong in geardum* young in the yard	*þone god sende* and God sent him
folce tó frófre the folk to prosper	*fyrenðearfe ongeat* after warring a long time	*þæt híe ǽr drugon* that they suffered
aldorléase being leaderless	*lange hwíle* for a long while.	*him þæs Líffréa* The Lord of Life
wudres wealdend and Glorious Almighty	*woroldáre forgeaf* granted him honour throughout the world	*Béowulf wæs bréme* Béowulf was noble
blǽdwíde sprang his glory became widespread,	*Scyldes eafera* Scyldes' heir,	*Scedelandum in* in the land of the Norse

Fig 3

DRAWINGS OF THE SEAX
SHORT SWORDS FOR
CLOSE IN FIGHTING

from 24" to 30"

The Frisians came from Frisia, the northern part of the present-day Netherlands, the north-west coastal region of Germany, south-west Jutland and all the small islands that run roughly parallel to the Dutch, German and Danish coastline. With this international overlap, the Frisians had the same Germanic tongue as the Jutes, Angles and Saxons, but once again with very different dialects.

The Franks came from an area south of the Frisians, including parts of the present-day Netherlands and Belgium. They were known as fierce fighters. The name *Frank* derives from the Old Germanic word *franca* meaning a 'javelin', which is believed to have been one of their favourite weapons in battle. The Franks did not join in the full Germanic invasion of the British shores, and only a few joined in with some spasmodic raiding and pillaging of the English east coast. Although some did settle, they did not play any significant role in the creation of the English language.

It is reasonable to assume that there would be dialectal differences within each group, just as there is in any other language. For instance, the northern Angles, because of their close proximity to the southern Jutes, would have some south Jutish dialect words in their vocabulary not known to the southern Angles, who themselves would have some northern Saxon dialect words as part of their everyday talk. It would also be very reasonable to assume that someone from the south Saxons would find it hard to understand a person from north Jutland, although they were speaking the same language. In the same way, someone speaking broad Cornish may find it difficult to comprehend broad Geordie, and vice versa.

Where did the first invaders land? The Jutes, led by the legendary Hengist and Horsa with Hengist's son Aesc, were the first to invade. At the Battle of Crecganford, in AD 465, they were victorious over the British kingdom of Cantware, modern-day Kent. However, Horsa was killed and Hengist became king of Kent. Eventually the Jutes would travel down the coast and establish the kingdom of Ynys Weith, on the present-day Isle of Wight and Hampshire coast, the latter to be jointly ruled with the West Saxons later.

The Angles invaded the east coast. Their first established settlement was called *Gypes Wic*, pronounced *yippes wich*, modern-day Ipswich; many historians argue that Ipswich is the oldest English settlement, with Colchester being the oldest recorded British settlement. The Angles conquered the eastern Britons and became known as the kingdom of the East Angles, present-day Norfolk, Suffolk and part of Cambridgeshire.

For over two hundred years, more and more Angles invaded the east coast and ventured further inland, especially along the main rivers and their tributaries. They gradually conquered further west and north, occupying great swathes of previously held Brythonic territory and establishing their own mighty Angle kingdoms.

Mercia was originally centred along the River Trent and most of its minor tributaries, which is today part of the East Midlands. The western boundary the Mercians had with the Britons determined their name. They called themselves *Myrce*, which translates as 'the border people'. Over time the kingdom of Mercia became all conquering and all powerful. They waged war against many other Angle kingdoms and annexed their territories. They also suppressed the Britons farther west, approximately as far as the current Welsh/English border.

ICELANDIC

THE DIFFERENT
GERMANIC LANGUAGE
SUB GROUPS OF THE
PRESENT DAY

FAROESE

SWEDISH

NORWEGIAN

DANISH

DUTCH

ENGLISH

GERMAN

FLEMISH

SWISS
GERMAN

AUSTRIAN

Map 5

The Middle Angles occupied modern Leicestershire and East Staffordshire and most likely went as far south as the Cambridgeshire Uplands and the Chilterns. They later became absorbed by the Mercians.

The Hwicce kingdom was established in AD 577 and took in parts of modern Worcestershire, Warwickshire and Gloucestershire. Some fifty years later, though, it was also annexed by Mercia.

The Deira kingdom was initially established along the River Derwent and eventually extended southwards from the River Tees to the Humber Estuary, and eastwards from the Vale of York to the sea. Deira would later merge with another Angle kingdom, Bernicia, to become a major power of the day.

The kingdom of Bernicia was north of the Deira domain and stretched from the River Tees into the south-eastern region of Scotland, evidenced with place names ending in *burgh* and *ton*, which are Angle suffixes for 'fortification' and 'farmstead' settlement respectively (for example, Edinburgh and Hamilton). Bernicia merged

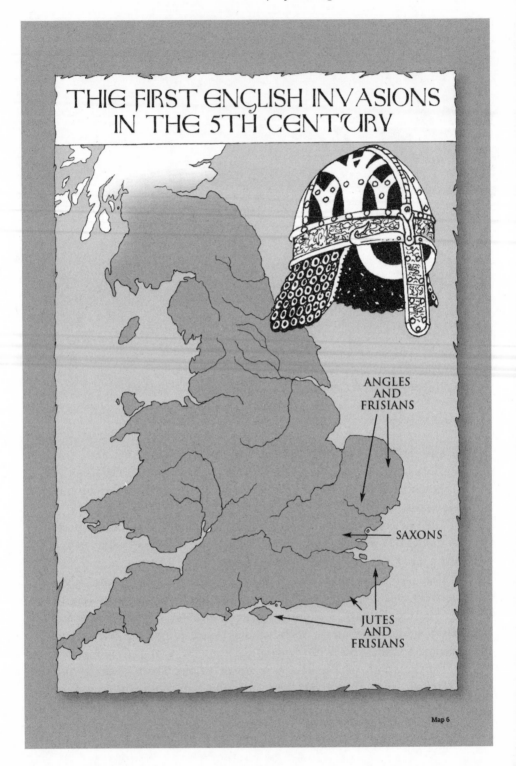

with Deira to create an *Engelisc* superpower north of the Humber, subsequently named Northumbria.

The Lindsey kingdom was comparatively small, being mainly Lincolnshire west of The Wash. This area was also annexed by Northumbria.

When the Angles were marauding their way through the countryside, the Saxons did so as well. They first conquered part of south-east Britain and then gradually moved westwards as far as the ancient British kingdom of Kernow, modern-day Cornwall. The Saxons then split their occupied territory into four: the East Saxons, the Middle Saxons, the West Saxons and the South Saxons, which ultimately became known as Essex, Middlesex, Wessex and Sussex respectively. They did attempt to annex land to the north of the East Saxons and try to create a territory to be known as the North Saxons. They waged a ferocious war against the East Angles, but the south folk of the East Angles (modern-day Suffolk) stood firm and the Saxons were thwarted.

The Saxons were a much smaller invading force than the Angles, yet throughout history the English are mainly referred to as Saxons: the Romans said *Saxonicum*, the Scots say *Sassenach* and the Welsh say *Saesneg*, all literally translated as 'Saxon'. Later, the Normans did actually recognise the Angle element and referred to the English as Anglo-Saxon.

The Frisians joined in this Germanic invasion of Britain too, mainly with the Angles that occupied East Anglia.

This conglomeration of all the invading pagan Germanic tribes would collectively become known as *Engelisc* (English), mainly due to the fact that the Angles were the biggest invading force. The second big factor was the input of King Alfred the Great, the ruler of the West Saxons, when he referred to all the Saxons and Angles in Britain as *Engelisc*. It is believed that he did this because the majority of the tribes at the time had been converted to Christianity and he wanted to separate himself, and distance himself, from his pagan Saxon cousins back in Europe. Alfred's use of the word *Engelisc* endorsed the name and gave credence to the land being called the 'Land of the Angles', *Englaland* or very rarely, *Englalanda*. The Germanic invasion was so overwhelming that the majority of place names in *Englaland* have *Engelisc* roots.

However, not all the Britons had been conquered by this Germanic mix. Cornwall and Devon were virtually untouched, as was Wales, Cumbria and the Strathclyde Welsh.

Spear →

TYPICAL 6-7TH CENTURY ANGLE WARRIOR

Helmet

Wolf Warrior
Banner

Wolf Pelt

Baldric for
Large Sword

Fascia Ventralis
(Cummberband)
Helps Prevent
Belts Chafing

Leather
Bag/Satchel

Small Sword

Axe Hammer

Leg Bindings

photograph courtesy of
Maria and "Wobbly" Legg

ill 1

These new *Engelisc* invading settlers had come in their hordes and practically overrun the place – so much so that they referred to the indigenous Britons as *walas* or *wealas*, which translates as 'strangers' or 'foreigners'. Many of the Britons were pushed westwards and subsequently two of the areas they settled became known as *Walas* (Wales) and *Cornwalas* (Cornwallis or Cornwall). The Britons that fled to present-day north-west France did so in such great numbers that the area became known as Brittany, and they themselves as Bretons. This forced migration led to a name change in AD 1136, when Geoffrey de Monmouth wanted to distinguish the Britons in Brittany from the ones in Britain. He referred to the larger of the two land masses as Great Britain, for the same reason there are Great and Little in many English village names. It appears more obvious in French with *Bretagne* (Brittany) and *Grande Bretagne*.

Contrary to popular belief, not all the Britons fled westwards from the all-conquering *Engelisc*. Many Britons succumbed and stayed behind. They were either taken into slavery or settled down, playing a subsidiary role to the *Engelisc*. Many of the Britons integrated fully into the culture, including marriage, and accepted the new way of life, even adopting the *Engelisc* language, which practically wiped out their British mother tongue. Only a few British or Brythonic words remained in their vocabulary.

Some of the Britons who stayed behind established their own settlements. The many places throughout England with Walton in the name generally derive from Old English *wala*, referring to the British 'strangers', plus *tun*, Old English for a farmland settlement. The villages that have Walsham in the name are derived from *wales ham*, which means a Briton's enclosure (*hamm*) or homestead settlement (*ham*). The places called Walworth derive their name from a Briton's enclosure (*wala worth*). The villages with Walden in the title refer to a valley, *denu*, inhabited by the *wealh*, the Britons. The several places with Bretton or Bretten in the name, including Monk Bretton, Yorkshire, and Brettenham, Norfolk, refer to a farmstead settlement, *ton*, belonging to Ancient Britons. There are many other place name examples which fully support the idea that a good number of Britons stayed behind and integrated into *Engelisc* ways and spoke the way of the *Engelisc*. Recent DNA testing has also proved that many of the Britons stayed behind and settled in with the *Engelisc*.

However, strangely enough, the surnames of Britain, Brittain, Britten and all its other variations do not refer to the Britons in Britain.

Examples of some *Engelisc* place names

Engelisc	meaning	Places	*Engelisc*	meaning	Places
ác	oak tree	Acle, Acton	æppel	apple tree	Appleford, Appleton
æsc	ash tree	Ashbury, Ashford	æspe	aspen tree	Aspenden, Aspull
ald	old	Aldbrough, Aldbury	alor	alder tree	Alderbury, Alderholt
bæce	stream	Backwell, Beccles	bēl	funeral pyre	Belaugh, Belsay
birce	birch tree	Birch, Birchanger	blæc	black	Blackburn, Blackpool
box	box tree	Boxgrove, Boxley	brād	broad	Broadstairs, Broadwas
brōc	brook	Brockham, Brockton	brocc	badger	Brockhall, Brockley
brōm	broom	Bromley, Brompton	bucc	buck	Buckden, Buckenham
bula	bull	Bulley, Bulmer	burh	fort	Burbage, Burgh
cald	cold	Caldecote, Caldwell	clæg	clay	Claydon, Clayhanger
clif	cliff	Cliffe, Cliffton	clopp	hill	Clophill, Clopton
cōl	coal	Coldred, Coldridge	denu	valley	Denford, Denham
deōp	deep	Depden, Deptford	deōr	deer	Dearham, Dereham
dīc	ditch	Diss, Ditchburn	dūn	hill	Dundon, Dundry
ēast	east	Eastbury, Eastchurch	ecg	edge	Edgefield, Edgworth
ēg	island	Eyam, Eye	elm	elm tree	Elmore, Elmton
feld	field	Heathfield, Heckfield	fenn	fen	Fenham, Fenton
fleax	flax	Flaxley, Flaxton	flēot	creek	Benfleet, Fleet
ford	ford	Fordham, Romford	fox	fox	Foxham, Foxholes
gāt	goat	Gatcombe, Gateshead	gōs	goose	Gosfield, Gosford
grafa	trench	Graveney, Redgrave	grēne	green	Greenham, Greenlaw
grēot	gravel	Greete, Greetham	hæcc	hatchgate	Hatch, Hatch End
hæsel	hazel	Hazelwood	hǣð	heath	Heathcote, Heathrow
hēah	high	Higham, Highbury	hēg	hay	Haydon, Hayfield
hōh	ridge	Hooe, Sutton Hoo	hol	hollow	Holcot, Holford
hrēod	reed	Rede, Redlynch	hwǣt	wheat	Wheatacre, Wheatley
hwit	white	Whitestone, Whitford	hyll	hill	Hildenborough
ingas	family	Framlingham	lacu	stream	Lacock, Lake
lamb	lamb	Lambeth, Lambley	lēah	clearing	Lee, Lees, Leigh
lind	lime tree	Lindridge, Lindsell	lýtel	little	Littleborough
mǣd	meadow	Medbourne, Meddon	mǣgden	maiden	Maidenhead, Maidford
mapel	maple	Mappleborough	mere	pool	Mere. Mersea
mersc	marsh	Marske, Marston	middel	middle	Middleton, Middlewich
mynster	minster	Minster, Westminster	oter	otter	Otterbourne, Otteton
peru	pear tree	Perivale, Perton	scēap	sheep	Shepshed, Shepton
scīr	shire	Cheshire, Wiltshire	stoc	outlying	Stoke Newington
strōd	marshy	Strood, Stroud	sūð	south	Southill, Sutton
weald	woodland	Waldron, Weald	worð	enclosure	Worthen, Worthing

Fig 4

The name refers to the Bretons from Brittany, as in the surname Brittney. They mainly came over as a large army of mercenaries with William the Conqueror in 1066. The variations of Brett and Breton have the same derivation as the surname Britain.

For two centuries or more the *Engelisc* tribes not only waged war on the Britons, who would not submit, but they also fought amongst themselves. The kingdoms of Mercia, Northumbria, East Anglia, Wessex and all the other kingdoms were warring factions causing boundary changes, takeovers, alliances, false alliances and a very unstable society. So unstable, in fact, that they were not in a position to properly defend their shores. The time was ripe for further invasions and more easy pickings.

The Danish and Norwegian Vikings were on their way!

4

The Vikings

The first question one must ask is, 'Who were the Vikings?' Initially, they were known as the Great Army of the Danes. Through time they became known as Vikings, a term for seafaring pirates who usually raided during the summer. Eventually it has become a generic term for all Scandinavians.

The Viking invasions commenced in AD 789 with the Norwegians off the Wessex coast on the Isle of Portland. The Danish Vikings also made numerous incursions around the coast for the next eighty years or so, including the sacking of the monastery at Lindisfarne in north-east England in 793. The Danes saw England as a vulnerable and plentiful target and continued to raid the coast and seize hoards of stolen treasure, especially from abbeys and monasteries.

However, 865 onwards saw a significant change of attitude from the Danes. They no longer saw England as a help-yourself treasure trove; they thought it was about time to conquer and settle. With this aim in mind they arrived with much larger invading armies and in 866 captured the Northumbrian stronghold *Eoforwic* (pronounced *eyorwic*). The Danes kept the same name, but in their own Scandinavian dialect pronounced it as *yorvik*, although they spelled it *Jorvic*. The English would in turn change the pronunciation to *yorwik*, which would eventually become York, as it is in the present day.

The Danish Vikings were indeed an impressive ferocious fighting unit and by 876 had conquered most of the English kingdoms. Alfred, king of the West Saxons in Wessex, was left hiding in the Somerset wetlands. But Alfred, a confirmed Christian, gradually regrouped and rallied his troops to raise a formidable army against the heathen Vikings. Although of Saxon blood, Alfred would refer to his people as

Engelisc, English, and not Saxon. It is thought that there are two main reasons for Alfred adopting the word *Engelisc:* firstly, as previously explained, to distinguish himself from his pagan European cousins, but secondly to help unite the Angles and Saxons against the Viking foe. By 878 he had started to push the Vikings back and defeated them at the Battle of Edington, in Wiltshire. He pushed and pushed until ten years later the Treaty of Wedmore was signed. This treaty established what has become known as the Danelaw and divided England in two halves: one half to be controlled by King Alfred and the English and the other half by the Vikings.

For approximately the next 200 years the Vikings and English would do battle with fortune favouring one and then the other. Alfred the Great's grandson, King Athelstan, would unite the whole of England under one English monarch for the first time ever. It is widely recognised by modern historians that Athelstan was the first king of all England. In fact, he practically succeeded in uniting the whole of the British Isles under one rule after his victory at the Battle of Brunanburh in 937. This ferocious conflict was fought between the victorious army of Athelstan, king of England and Wales, against the combined forces of an alliance between Olaf Guthfrithson, king of Dublin, Constantine, king of Scotland, and Owen, king of Strathclyde.

Much later, in 1018, the Danish king Cnut (Canute) would seize control of England and most of the British Isles. This to-ing and fro-ing would carry on until 1066 when everything changed yet again.

The Vikings had a big effect on spoken English and influenced a number of English dialects, particularly those in the north. The names of many villages, towns and cities with Viking roots will readily support this theory. Furthermore, many Viking names would eventually become established as English surnames after 1066. However, it was not until the twentieth century that it was really appreciated how big the Scandinavian influence had been. The Vikings, in particular the Danes, eventually became one of the biggest invading forces to settle in England, second only to the Angles. It has therefore been suggested in some quarters that it would be more accurate to say that the English are mainly Anglo-Viking rather than Anglo-Saxon.

During the time of this Anglo-Viking interaction, the language of the English became more streamlined. The Vikings spoke the same language as the English, although in vastly different dialects, but there is no record of interpreters ever being used during the various negotiations and treaties. Therefore, to help understand one another they would both quite naturally simplify their phrases and their grammar.

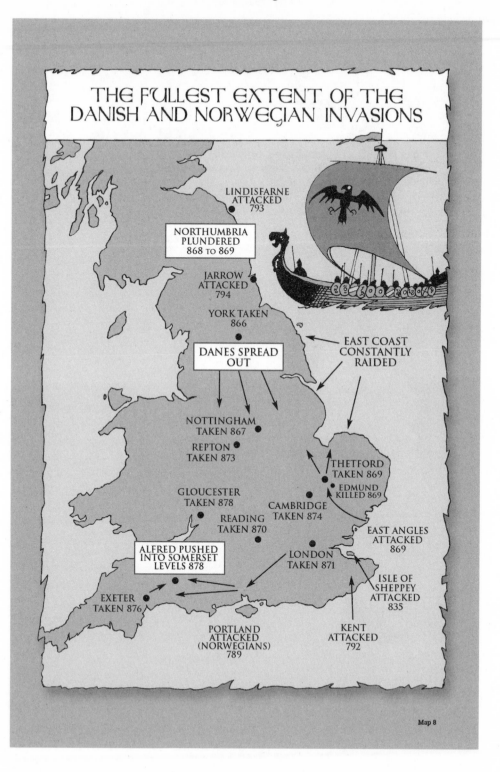

THE FULLEST EXTENT OF THE
DANISH AND NORWEGIAN INVASIONS

LINDISFARNE
ATTACKED
793

NORTHUMBRIA
PLUNDERED
868 TO 869

JARROW
ATTACKED
794

YORK TAKEN
866

EAST COAST
CONSTANTLY
RAIDED

DANES SPREAD
OUT

NOTTINGHAM
TAKEN 867

REPTON
TAKEN 873

THETFORD
TAKEN 869

EDMUND
KILLED 869

GLOUCESTER
TAKEN 878

CAMBRIDGE
TAKEN 874

READING
TAKEN 870

EAST ANGLES
ATTACKED
869

ALFRED PUSHED
INTO SOMERSET
LEVELS 878

LONDON
TAKEN 871

ISLE OF
SHEPPEY
ATTACKED
835

EXETER
TAKEN 876

PORTLAND
ATTACKED
(NORWEGIANS)
789

KENT
ATTACKED
792

Map 8

This practice would eventually become commonplace, as can be seen in the formation of plurals. Old English principles were very complicated and depended on whether a noun was strong or weak and whether masculine, feminine or neuter. Many other rules had to be applied as well, and as a result there were several ways of creating a plural.

In many cases, however, they simply added an -s or -es to the end of the word. But other rules applied such as adding -um to the noun as a suffix; another way was to change the spelling, or just leave it the same as the singular; another method would be to add -en as a suffix and sometimes -a or -ru. These are just a few examples of the different ways of making plurals in Old English, which illustrate how complicated it must have been. It is easy to see why there were so many regional variations.

The Danes, although having the same Germanic linguistic roots as Old English, had created a different and equally complex system for their plural nouns.

With the Anglo-Saxons and Vikings living alongside one another, and eventually integrating, human nature would take its course and the more simple method would prevail. Although not quite universal, adding an -s or -es to change the singular into a plural was largely adopted by all the English-speaking people, and endorsed by the Normans after 1066. However, the pronunciation of the plural -s was inconsistent and would vary from either a *zz* sound, as in 'boys', 'girls' and 'hands', or a *ss* sound as in 'cats', 'boats' and 'books'.

There are quite a few exceptions where the Old English methods held fast and are evident in Standard English today. By adding -en as a suffix the following plurals are created: children, oxen and brethren, although the latter more commonly gives way to brothers today. The plurals of man and woman are changed to men and women respectively, but -mans is used when talking about humans, Romans and Normans rather than *humen, Romen* and *Normen*, yet -men in firemen, postmen and policemen. There are still some regional leftovers in dialects with -en and -n plural nouns, such as *shoen* for shoes and *housen* for houses. It is also thought that the phrase 'dressed up to the nines' is a corruption of 'dressed up to thine eyen', which translates as 'dressed up to the eyes'.

Changing the spelling rather than adding an s still exists with, for example, mice, geese and teeth; and changing the *f* to *v* in knives, wives and hooves, although the *f* in hoofs, turfs and dwarfs is acceptable;

English Plurals

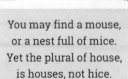

We'll begin with a box,
and the plural is boxes.
But the plural of ox,
became oxen not oxes.

One fowl is a goose,
but two are called geese.
Yet the plural of moose,
should never be meese.

You may find a mouse,
or a nest full of mice.
Yet the plural of house,
is houses, not hice.

If the plural of man,
is always called men.
Why shouldn't the plural,
of pan be called pen?

If I spoke of my foot,
and show you my feet,
and I give you a boot,
would a pair be beet?

If one is a tooth,
a whole set are teeth.
Why can't the plural
of booth be beeth?

Then one may be that,
and three would be those.
Yet hat in the plural,
would never be hose.
The plural of cat,
would never be cose.

We speak of a brother,
and also of brethren.
But though we say mother,
we never say methren.

So plurals in English,
I think you'll agree.
Are indeed very tricky,
singularly !

Anon

Fig 5

keeping the spelling the same for both singular and plural nouns still remains, for example in 'deer', 'fish' and 'sheep'.

The grammatical system of having inanimate objects with gender, namely masculine, feminine and neuter, started to disappear with the Danes and English trying to converse with one another. This again helped to make the English language become grammatically easier. Previously, the gender not only determined the spelling of the noun but also any adjectives and associated words. By dispensing with gender the grammar generally became more consistent and easier to understand. However, it has remained common practice to refer to some objects and items as male and female. For example, the planet is referred to as 'Mother Earth' and countries tend to be female as well, although 'fatherland' refers to the land of one's fathers. When a boat is launched, reference is made to 'all that sail in her' and motorcars and motorbikes are referred to as female, as in 'take her for a spin'. There are many other examples.

The Viking streamlining meant that English grammar would eventually become one of the simplest in Europe, although it would also remain one of the most difficult to learn because of the numerous inconsistencies in pronunciation.

The foundation stones of the English language were well in place by the time the Normans arrived in 1066.

5

The Normans

Who were the Normans? What language did they speak? Who did they bring with them to England in 1066?

The Normans were originally bands of pirates from Norway in the ninth and tenth centuries. They were known as *Northmen*, 'men from the north', and they regularly sacked, pillaged and plundered the coastal areas of northern France during the summer months and returned home to Norway for the winter. On one occasion they sailed up the River Seine as far as Paris. It was not until the early part of the tenth century when there was a change of plan by the *Northmen*. Rollo, also known as *Ganger Hrolfr*, decided that they should start to settle and create permanent Viking communities. This they did by invading and settling in an area of present-day northern France that would eventually be named after them: Normandy. This part of France had been occupied by the Franks, a Germanic tribe from northern Europe, and the northern French dialect was heavily inflected with this Germanic input. So influential were the Franks throughout the land that modern-day France is actually named after them. France was not a unified country during this period but a mixture of many smaller kingdoms, including Burgundy, the kingdom of the Franks and the kingdom of the Visigoths. Therefore they did not have a standard French tongue. Rollo's Vikings accepted the structure of the language they found in that part of northern France but added some of their own words to its vocabulary.

Over one hundred years later, William became duke of Normandy and formed an alliance with Flanders. To cement this alliance he married into their royal household and tied the knot with Matilda of Flanders. William had a tenuous claim to the English throne, being

photograph courtesy of Maria and "Wobbly" Legg

first cousin once removed from Edward the Confessor, whose mother was Emma of Normandy.

William, Duke of Normandy, successfully invaded in 1066 and brought over a rich and mixed language. His own army's French dialect would have been the result of a northern French, Frankish and Viking hybrid. He brought with his invading forces a large contingent from Matilda's homeland, Flanders, who would have spoken another Germanic language, Flemish. William also employed French mercenaries from other parts of France, especially the Bretons from Brittany. After the Conquest some troops went home, but many stayed and settled.

William would have been referred to as *Guillaume* by the French element of his troops, and *Willelm* by the Viking and Germanic elements. The latter variation is actually seen on the Bayeux Tapestry.

Under the Normans the spoken word in England became a three-tier system. Royalty, the noble ruling classes and administrators would speak in their unique Franco-German mix, which later became known as Anglo-Norman French, or just Norman-French, whilst the vast majority of the population were English (that is, Anglo-Saxon or Anglo-Viking) and continued to use their native tongue. Latin was still the official language of the ecclesiastical caste and in formal education. This is borne out in the Norman-French and Latin recordings of many of the English place names in the Domesday Book, compiled in 1086, instead of the English spoken versions.

The Normans were very few in number compared with the English masses, but they were firmly in control. They tended to be large landowning barons with armies, part of the ecclesiastic hierarchy and political administrators. Although the Norman aristocracy continued to use Anglo-Norman French, they accepted the structure of the English language they found, but added a few thousand words to the vocabulary. The Norman input into the English language would have a profound effect and started the period known as Middle English. During this time the English language would be streamlined even more into an English tongue that can be recognised in the modern form we have today.

The Norman three-tier system was evident for roughly 350 years, and would finally end in the early 1400s during the House of Lancaster's dynasty, at the time of the Hundred Years' War.

The Normans also introduced the concept of hereditary surnames, which primarily took the form of either Viking warrior nicknames, French place names or some French nicknames. The name William

BAYEUX
TAPESTRY

ill 2

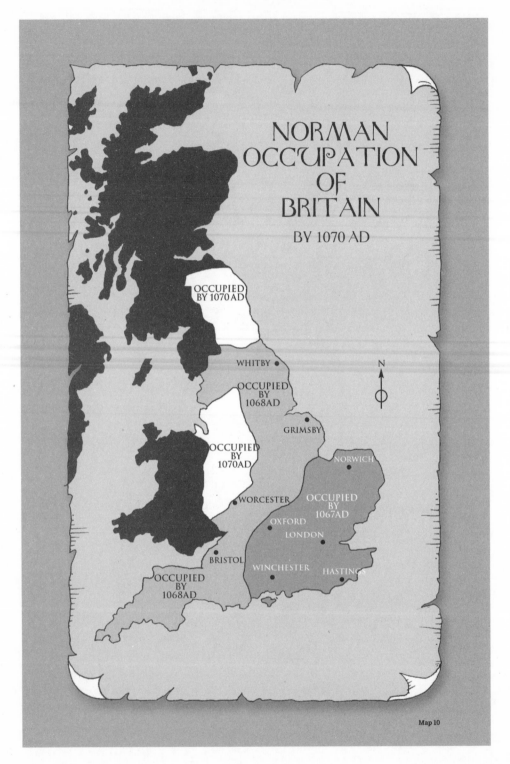

itself derives from Willhelm, which is a Viking-Germanic warrior nickname for 'wolf helmet'. The warrior wearing a helmet with a wolf engraving would most probably lead the troops into battle.

Through time the English, with their Anglo-Saxon and Viking mix, would fall in line and adopt surnames that reflected their own linguistic background. Even today, analysis of surnames and place names can determine which ones are Anglo-Saxon, which are Viking-based and which are Norman. Research into place names can also help in ascertaining the extent and depth of each invading force that came to the British shores.

The second most famous book in English history, second only to The Bible, is undoubtedly the two volumes of the *Domesday Book*. These were practically a complete census of England and part of Wales, and have become a great and invaluable source for English historians and historical analysts. The *Little Domesday* covered present-day East Anglia and Essex and the *Great Domesday* covered most of the rest of the country. However, some lands in the north of England, present-day Cumbria, Durham and Northumberland, were not covered for two reasons: firstly, not all of the North had been conquered yet by the Normans; and secondly, the Bishop of Durham had exclusive rights over some of the area for purposes of taxation. The city of London along with Winchester and some other towns were not included because they had been granted tax exemption.

During the gathering of the census the Norman scribes used a Vernacular Latin, but when recording English place names they invariably resorted to Norman-French. The surnames of the landowning Normans were also transcribed in this massive document and, for the first time ever, a few English surnames were also recorded. Most English surnames, however, would be recorded later in documents such as the Curia Regis Rolls, Assize Rolls, Subsidy Rolls and similar, as more and more of the English adopted hereditary surnames.

How did the Norman's rich heritage of languages and dialects affect spoken English?

The Normans had a massive influence on spoken English – eventually, that is. Their Norman-French dialect was evident in both their writing and in their speech, but it took time to filter through to the English-speaking masses. The Normans did not have much regard for the English language and saw it as being colloquial, rustic and for the uneducated. They saw it as a spoken barbaric language, largely pre-literate with only a few examples of the written word, as in the *Anglo-Saxon Chronicle*. The Normans considered the English

Examples of surnames
of Scandinavian origin

surname	Old Norse	meaning	surname	Old Norse	meaning
Allgood	*Algot*	battle Geat*	Arkell	*Arnkell*	eagle helmet
Osborn	*Ásbiǫrn*	god bear	Osgood	*Ásgautr*	god Geat*
Barne	*Bjiǫrn*	warrior	Bond	*Bóndi*	peasant
Brand	*Brandr*	firebrand	Dolphin	*Dólgfinnr*	battle scar
Ayloffe	*Elaf*	noble gift	Farman	*Farmann*	fair man
Finn	*Finnr*	fair hair	Fiske	*Fiskr*	fisherman
Gambell	*Gamall*	old	Gooderam	*Guðrum*	battle snake
Goodhew	*Guðhugi*	battle mind	Grime	*Grímr*	fierce
Grimmet	*Grímhildr*	war helmet	Gunn	*Gunnr*	battle
Gunnell	*Gunnildr*	battle fierce	Havelock	*Hafleikr*	seaport
Raven	*Hrafn*	raven	Rankill	*Hrafnkell*	raven kettle
Kettle	*Ketill*	cauldron	Knott	*Knútr*	knot
Orme	*Ormr*	snake	Randolph	*Rannulfr*	shield wolf
Simmonds	*Sigmundr*	protector	Stein	*Steinn*	stone
Storey	*Stóri*	large	Swannell	*Svanhildr*	swan battle
Swain	*Sveinn*	herdsman	Thorold	*Þóraldr*	Thor ruler
Turpin	*Þorfinnr*	Thor fair	Thurgood	*Þorgautr*	Thor Geat*
Thurgar	*Þorgeirr*	Thor spear	Thurkell	*Þorkell*	Thor kettle
Tooke	*Tóki*	abbr of Thurkell	Tooley	*Tóli*	Thor relic
Triggs	*Tryggr*	faithfull	Ulph	*Úlfr*	wolf

* Geat – Scandinavian tribe of Beowulf

Fig 6

Examples of surnames of Norman origin

surname	Norman-French	meaning	surname	Norman-French	meaning
Ames	*amis*	friend	Angers	from Angers, France	
Bailey	*bailli*	chief magistrate	Barker	*barcher*	shepherd
Beauchamp	from Beauchamps, France		Beaumont	from Beaumont, France	
Bell	*bel*	beautiful	Bennett	*Beniet*	little Ben
Bloomfield	from Blonville, France		Butcher	*bouchier*	butcher
Chandler	*candelier*	candlemaker	Clement	*clement*	merciful
Deacon	*deacon*	church official	De Vere	from Ver, Normandy	
Double	*doublel*	a twin	Durrant	*durant*	obstinate
Foster	*fustrier*	forester	Fletcher	*flecher*	arrow maker
Grainger	*grangier*	estate manager	Gross	*gros*	big, fat
Latimer	*latinier*	interpreter	Lovell	*lovel*	wolf cub
Mariner	*marinier*	sailor	Mercer	*mercer*	merchant
Noble	*noble*	noble	Page	*page*	attendant
Parker	*parquier*	estate guard	Parmenter	*parmentier*	tailor
Palmer	*palmer*	pilgrim	Proctor	*proketour*	manager
Rickard	*ricard*	Richard	Summers	*somier*	sumpter
Spencer	*despencier*	food seller	Squirrel	*esquerel*	squirrel
Scrivener	*escrivain*	writer	Tabram	*tabourner*	drummer
Taylor	*tailleur*	tailor	Tennant	*tenant*	tenant
Vaisey	*envoisie*	playful	Vine	*vigne*	worker at a vineyard

Fig 7

Examples of surnames
of Old English origin

surname	Old English	meaning	surname	Old English	meaning
Adlem	*Æðelhelm*	Elf helmet*	Aldred	*Æðelrǣd*	Elf counsel*
Allston	*Ǣelstān*	Elf stone*	Baker	*bæcere*	baker
Bicker	*bēocere*	bee keeper	Bullman	*bula mann*	bull keeper
Calvert	*calf hierde*	calf herd	Chapman	*cēapmann*	merchant
Cobbold	*cūðbeald*	famous bold	Eldridge	*Ælfrīc*	Elf ruler*
Elsay	*Ælfsige*	Elf victory*	Fox	*fox*	cunning
Fry	*frīg*	freeborn	Fulcher	*folchere*	foot soldier
Goodwin	*gōd wine*	good friend	Grimwood	*grimweard*	helmet guard
Groom	*grom*	manservant	Harper	*hearpere*	harp player
Hunt	*hunta*	hunter	Knight	*cniht*	servant
Little	*lȳtel*	little	Mower	*māwan*	to mow
Rooke	*hrōc*	rook	Roper	*rāp*	rope
Seager	*sǣgār*	sea spear	Seeley	*sǣlig*	holy, blessed
Shanks	*sceanca*	leggy	Small	*smœl*	small, thin
Smith	*smyð*	smith	Speller	*spellian*	a speaker
Stannard	*stānheard*	stone hard	Stark	*stearc*	firm, harsh
Todd	*todde*	like a fox	Tyler	*tigele*	tile
Ward	*weard*	guard	Webb	*webbe*	weaver
Wheeler	*hwēol*	wheel	Woodward	*wud weard*	wood keeper
Woolnough	*wulfnōð*	wolf boldness	Young	*geong*	young

* Ælf in Anglo-Saxon mythology was almost a semi–god
and meant noble in a name

Fig 8

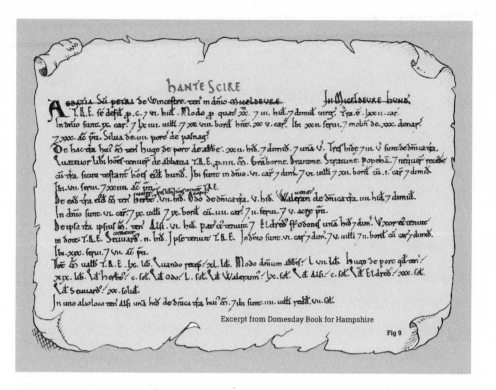

Excerpt from Domesday Book for Hampshire

Fig 9

language as the word of the peasant and totally devoid of any structured grammar. Therefore the Normans continued to use their Norman-French tongue, with Latin being used in the Church and in the legal profession. As far as the Normans were concerned, English was relegated to third place and largely ignored.

It is fair to say that the native English and the Norman invaders did not get on well together. The Conquest was brutal and cruel; although vastly outnumbered, the Normans were organised and extremely ruthless in imposing their authority and power throughout the land. Through time, however, with more and more of the English hierarchy showing allegiance and support to the king, and with more Normans and English intermarrying, things slowly started to converge and change; but the English-speaking people, then some 90 to 95 per cent of the population, maintained their English tongue and continued to uphold the structure of the language, although mainly as spoken word and with many regional variations.

In time, the Normans themselves would introduce around 10,000 words from their own dialect into the English vocabulary, many of which are part and parcel of Modern English today. Many of

Examples of some Norman words adopted into English

Norman	Modern English	Norman	Modern English	Norman	Modern English
hable	able	aide	aid	annuel	annual
apetit	appetite	armee	army	armure	armour
archier	archer	art	art	autorité	authority
bacon	bacon	bataille	battle	beauté	beauty
boef	beef	bescuit	biscuit	blond(e)	blond
bote	boot	carre	car	chaiere	chair
chambre	chamber	chapitre	chapter	charité	charity
cité	city	clos	close	colour	colour
commencier	commence	conceler	conceal	continuer	continue
cuntree	country	corage	courage	demandé	demand
disengager	disengage	desir	desire	destruire	destroy
diviner	divine	encontrer	encounter	enemí	enemy
engager	engage	fait	feat	fin	fine
forfet	forfeit	frire	fry	goune	gown
garde	guard	herb	herb	enfant	infant
joel	jewel	journee	journey	jus	juice
juree	jury	juste	just	justise	justice

Fig 10 I

Examples of some Norman words adopted into English

Norman	Modern English	Norman	Modern English	Norman	Modern English
labourer	labourer	langage	language	liberté	liberty
livree	livery	mansion	mansion	masson	mason
Mai	May	mesure	measure	marchandise	merchandise
marchant	merchant	mirour	mirror	moneie	money
moton	mutton	obeir	obey	odour	odour
peintour	painter	pardun	pardon	partir	part
pais	peace	paisent	peasant	poeple	people
prenance	pernancy	place	place	plague	plague
poure	poor	porc	pork	pouletrie	poultry
poeir	power	prove	proof	pourchacier	purchase
question	question	real	real	rostir	roast
saussiere	saucer	seel	seal	espice	spice
serf	serf	servant	servant	soldier	soldier
estai	stay	table	table	taillour	tailor
travail	travel	oncle	uncle	us	use
vassal	vassal	vaute	vault	veel	veal
venesoun	venison	verai	very	waitier	wait

Fig 10 II

these words originally related to officialdom and are evident in the vocabulary surrounding administration, parliament, government, the legal profession and the Crown. It followed on that more and more words would then filter down into everyday matters, including food production and various other trades.

The Normans introduced words beginning with, *con-, de-, dis-* and *en-*, such as conceal, continue, demand, encounter, disengage and engage. They also had words ending in, *-age, -ence,* and *-tion,* as in advantage, courage, language and commence; even more French words from other parts of France would in time become part of the vocabulary, thanks to the Normans' cousins, the Plantagenets from Anjou. Great swathes of France were under the control of the English monarch.

Middle English, 1066–1487

This is where the fun begins! Up until now spoken English was well established with many regional differences; a standard, unified form of the language had not even been considered. After the Norman invasion England became a linguistic melting pot as the English language took another evolutionary step. It is fair to say that by the end of the Middle English period, the written word had evolved into a language that can be recognised as very similar to the English we know today. During this period, distinct regional dialects would emerge and perhaps the foundations of a Standard English would be established. These linguistic precursors would take a number of centuries to become fully apparent, but once established they would develop into the predominant language of the world.

The exact dates of the start and finish of the Middle English period are historically contested and discussed, with historians putting forward various timescales. The most logical timescale would be from the Norman Conquest, in 1066, to the end of the Wars of the Roses, in 1487. This latter date also coincides with the introduction of the printing press into England – an invention that would not only promote literature written in English on a grand scale but would also help to fertilise those embryonic seeds for a Standard English to grow and flourish at a later date.

The three-tier hierarchy of language use would survive until the reign of Henry V, when it would finally disappear. The ordinary folk of England would maintain their dialectal native English tongues, whilst royalty, along with the noble ruling classes, people at court, the ecclesiastical hierarchy and administrators spoke Norman-French. But gradually that would all change to practically 'full English' in the early 1400s. In fact, at the Battle of Agincourt, in 1415, Henry V would have addressed his troops in either an English dialect or even perhaps the emerging new Chancery English.

Evidence of the three-tier system can be seen in manuscripts that record many of the English place names that are divided into Great and Little. The Norman-French-speaking clerics would write these down as *Magna* and *Parva* respectively as a description after the place name, whilst the general English-speaking public would use Great and Little as an adjective before the name.

There are many instances of the *Magna* and *Parva* recordings during this period, one example being *Dalby Magna* and *Dalby Parva* in Leicestershire, which would become Great and Little Dalby respectively. There are scores of other examples up and down the country. However, there were also the odd exceptions which proved the rule and perhaps were an indication of a shift from Norman-French to English by the administrators. In 1198 Great and Little Brickhill in Buckinghamshire were written down as *Magna Brikehille* and *Parva Brichull* respectively, instead of *Brikehille Magna* and *Brichull Parva*. Another 'Great' example is the fact that King John's Great Charter in 1215 would become known as the *Magna Carta*, and not *Carta Magna*. Gradually the English would get their way, but a few places today maintain the Norman-French descriptions, such as Thornham Magna and Thornham Parva in Suffolk.

Through time more kings of England gradually moved over to using English as their first language, and the society around them would copy and change accordingly. In 1399 Henry IV took his oath in English, and it is thought that he spoke no Norman-French at all. His son Henry V finally put an end to the by then antique three-tier system in 1413, when he decreed that English should completely take over from Norman-French in government and court. It was also during Henry V's reign that a uniform Chancery English would evolve and come to be used in political and bureaucratic circles. However, Latin would continue to be used by the Church, and Norman-French and Latin would be used in the legal system.

The medieval miracle, mystery and history plays, along with the pageants, would help keep the English language alive and help break down the three-tier system. During the 1300s and for the next two hundred years there were many English towns and cities that put on these extravagant early forms of English open-air theatre.

Originally, the plays would take place on particular religious Christian feast and holy days. Plays around Corpus Christi Day, in early June, were the most popular and Whitsuntide performances were fairly common, too, but there were also a number of shows during other festivals. The travelling performers would be male and number only two or three at the most. They would set up a temporary stage somewhere prominent in the town, like the market square. The script would be in English.

The plot would normally be based on a religious theme and an elaboration of a Biblical story; sometimes the theme would be that of Saint George and the dragon. These forms of entertainment were extremely popular and would be performed in front of large audiences from all walks of life.

The style of play soon developed along two different avenues: the cycles and the pageants. A cycle was peculiar to England and described the cycle of man through various stages, from Adam to the Resurrection of Christ, from Creation to the Day of Judgement. The towns most famous for regularly performing the cycles were Chester, York, Coventry, Wakefield, Lincoln, Newcastle and Canterbury and even came to have cycles named after them, for instance the York Cycle. Each different stage of the cycle would be financed by a guild – for example, the three kings could be sponsored by the goldsmiths' guild and the shipbuilding guild would more often than not finance the cycle relating to Noah's Ark. The guilds were advertising their wares to all and sundry and wanted to put on a good show in front of a guaranteed huge audience.

Plays regularly lasted three days or more and the town would close for the duration. All shops were instructed to close, all noisy work was banned and townsfolk were expected to attend. Armed guards were used to ensure the general safety of those attending, an early form of crowd control. Large numbers of the population were listening to plays written in English.

A complete cycle would ordinarily be the work of more than one playwright, and a number of scriptwriters would get together to produce each part of the cycle. Although the standards of penmanship would vary greatly, it still meant that English and not Norman-French was being circulated and listened to by the masses, and the endorsement and credibility of spoken English was taking hold in a big way.

Many of the actors would have the same part to play year after year, and very often obtained a nickname that was appropriate to that part. A number of English surnames have derived from those cycle nicknames, such as Death and Farrer (Pharaoh).

The Thirde Pageante of Noye's Fludd

And firste in some high place or in the clowdes
if it may bee God speaketh unto Noe
standinge without the arke with all his familye

1

I God that all this world hath wrought
heaven and yearth and all of nought
I see my people in deede and thought
are sett fowle in sinne

2

My goost shall not lenge in mone
that through flesbe-likinge is my fone
but tyll six score yeares be commen
and gone to looke if the will blynne

3

Man that I made will I distroye
beast worme and fowle to flye
for on yearth the doe mee noye
the folke that are theron

4

Hit hammes mec so hurtfullye
the malice that doth now multiplye
that sore it greeves mee inwardlye
that ever I have mon

5

Therfore Noe my servante free
that righteous man arte as I see
a shippe sonne thou shalt make thee
of trees drye and light

6

Little chambers therin thou make
and bindinge sliche alsoe thou take
within and without thou ne slake
to annoynte yt through all thy might

7

Three hundreth cubitts yt shalbee longe
and fiftye broade to make it stronge
of height sixtye The meete thou fonge
thus measure thou hit aboute

8

One window worke through thy witt
a cubytt of length and breadc make hit
Upon the syde a doore shall shutte
for to corn in and owt

9

Eatinge-places thou make alsoe
three rowfed chambers one or too
for with water I thinke to flowe
mone that I make

10

Destroyed all they worlde shalbe
save thou thy wyfe thy sonnes three
and theme wyves alsoe with thee
shall fall before thy face

Fig 11

The pageants took their name from a type of cart, a pageant wagon. These lengthy plays were a progression from the stationary cycles played on a fixed stage, and were a sight to behold. Each pageant wagon would have its own set stage for each part of the cycle. The audience would be static and the play would gradually be performed in front of them as each wagon would roll away once it had finished, only for the next one to follow on. These were lavish affairs because the guilds continued to be the financial backers. Each wagon was sponsored by its own guild, and each, as before, wanted to make an impression when advertising their products. Underneath the wagon the actors would change their costumes and above would be the stage. The whole affair became such an extravaganza that the word 'pageant' gradually took on its meaning today.

The pageants gradually moved away from Biblical themes, and plays became ribald and rude and far removed from their original intention of performing religious stories in English to an English audience. Objections came from both the Roman Catholic Church and from those starting to break away from Catholicism; the guilds also started to object at this time and wanted to withdraw their financial support. Eventually, pageants were banned by Henry VIII, but made a brief comeback during the time of Mary when she allowed them to be performed again, although not to the same extent as previously. During Elizabeth's reign the writing was on the wall and pageants gradually petered out. This type of entertainment gave way to the rise of a much more formal English theatre, influenced by the Renaissance, with emerging Elizabethan writers such as Marlowe and Shakespeare.

The abandonment of the three-tier system was also helped greatly by Geoffrey Chaucer and other Middle English writers such as John Wycliffe, John Gower, Miles Coverdale, William Langland, Julian of Norwich and John Lydgate.

Geoffrey Chaucer (1340–1400) is without doubt the most famous of these wordsmiths from the Middle English period. His *The Canterbury Tales* has been read and studied throughout the ages ever since and translated into many languages throughout the world. This iconic volume of Middle English literature, along with his other works such as *Troilus and Criseyde*, are examples of how a vernacular spoken and written English were breaking through into the Norman-French-speaking elite. Up until that time it was considered both formally correct and fashionable to produce written works in Norman-French, which would be read or listened

Geoffrey Chaucer

Fig 12

to at the royal courts by the courtiers and their followers. Chaucer helped turn the tide.

Chaucer's brilliant writing would enthral and entertain the kings and their royal entourages at court for quite a number of years. English was starting to become more popular and in vogue and was held in greater regard than hitherto. Further, English was more expressive than Norman-French and possessed a richer range of vocabulary. It was more flexible in its interpretation and meaning, which allowed more wit and humour to be incorporated into written works. It also allowed authors to sometimes write in a raunchy and suggestive fashion that appealed to many at court, including the monarchs of the day and their royal followers.

In the absence of a standard form of the language, it is obvious to scholars of spoken English that Chaucer wrote his great works using a London dialect. On the other hand, John Lydgate, a prolific author in his time, would write in an East Anglian dialect; William Langland's epic poem *Piers Plowman* was written in his West Midland dialect; and Miles Coverdale's writings and Biblical translations would reflect his Yorkshire upbringing.

However, it would be the London dialect of Chaucer that would become the cornerstone of the first effort at a standardised English language. It was to become known as Chancery English, or Chancery Standard. This first attempt would be largely unsuccessful although it did play a small part in the development of a more unified language later on. The civil service and government bureaucracy needed to have a standardised written form of English that would readily be understood and recognised throughout the land. Perhaps more importantly, it created a standardised English that would ensure less ambiguity when drawing up official documents, decrees and manuscripts. This would lessen the chances of misinterpretation and reduce the opportunities for dispute and conflict.

Chancery Standard had been formulated between 1413 and 1422 during the reign of Henry V and was almost a finished article by the mid-1400s. London was the administrative centre of the country, which gave its dialect an immediate influence on the emerging version of the English language. Chancery Standard was spoken on official business and matters of state. It was written in official documents, manuscripts, decrees, royal charters and so on. However, the Church maintained its use of Latin, as decreed from Rome, whilst the legal profession continued to use a little Norman-French and some Latin, a practice which it has continued up to the present day.

Henry V had not specified any particular standard version; he only decreed that English should be used in government and at the royal court. There was no official edict or royal proclamation that insisted on the specific or general use of Chancery Standard. It was gradually spread around the country by court officials, government bureaucrats and administrators when on government business, royal affairs and matters of state. Because of this, in time Chancery Standard acquired an air of elitism, with a distinctly snobbish attitude amongst its clique of speakers.

The formation of Chancery English during the Middle English period saw spectacular alterations in pronunciation and wholesale changes to the grammar. The spelling of words became a little more uniform during this time, a standardisation helped by the unveiling of the new printing press in the late fifteenth century by William Caxton.

Caxton was an English diplomat, scholar, entrepreneur, writer and printer. He introduced printing into England after he had seen it in operation first hand in northern Europe and after successfully setting up a printing press himself in Bruges. It was here, in 1473, where Caxton published the first ever book to be printed in English. His own translation, it was entitled *Recuyell of the Historyes of Troye*. The book was so popular and such a success that Caxton decided to branch out and set up shop in Westminster, London, in 1476. The first book he printed in that same year was Geoffrey Chaucer's racy *The Canterbury Tales*.

Although Chancery Standard created a form of English that was more readily understood throughout the length and breadth of the land, there were still very distinct regional differences – so many that Chancery Standard could not be classified as Standard English. That would come much later. But it was a start!

MILLER'S
TALE

Literal translation of opening lines of Chaucer's Miller's Tale

Whilom ther was dwellynge at Oxenford
Once there was dwelling at Oxenford

A riche gnof, that gestes heeld to bord,
A rich countryman, that guests healthy to board,

And of his craft he was a carpenter.
And of his craft he was a carpenter.

With hym ther was dwellynge a poure scoler,
With him there was dwelling a poor scholar,

Hadde lerned art, but all his fantasye
Had learned art, but all his fantasy

Was turned for to lerne astrologye,
Was turned for to learn astrology,

And koude a certeyn of conclusions,
And knew a certain of conclusions,

To demen by interrogaciouns,
To agree by interrogations,

If that men asked hym, in certein houres
If that men asked him in certain hours

Whan that men sholde have droghte or elles shoures,
When that men should have drought or else showers,

Or if men asked hym what sholde bifalle
Or if men asked him what should befall

Of every thyng; I may nat rekene hem alle.
Of everything; I may not reckon them all.

This clerk was cleped hende Nicholas.
This scholar was called clever Nicholas.

Of deerne love he koude and of solas;
Of secret love he knew and of solace;

And therto he was sleigh and ful privee,
And thereto he was sly and full privy,

And lyk a mayden meke for to see.
And like a maiden meek for to see.

A chambre hadde he in that hostelrye
A chamber had he in that hostelry

Allone, withouten any compaignye,
Alone, without any company,

Ful fetisly ydight with herbes swoote;
Full elegantly prepare with herbs sweet;

And he hymself as sweete as is the roote
And he himself as sweet as is the root

Fig 13

Literal translation of opening lines of Chaucer's Miller's Tale

Of lycorys or of any cetewale.
Of licorice or of any zedoary.

His Almageste, and bookes grete and smale,
His Almageste, and books great and small,

His astrelabie, longynge for his art,
His astrolabe, belonging to his art,

His augrym stones layen faire apart,
His counting stones lay fair apart,

On shelves couched at his beddes heed;
On shelves arranged at his bed's head;

His presse ycovered with a faldyng reed;
His press covered with woollen blanket red;

And al above ther lay a gay sautrie,
And all above there lay a gay psaltery,

On which he made a-nyghtes melodie
On which he made a night melody

So swetely that all the chambre rong;
So sweetly that all the chamber rang;

And Angelus ad virginem he song;
And 'Angel to the Virgin' he sang;

And after that he song the Kynges Noote,
And after that he sang the King's Note,

Ful often blessed was his myrie throte,
Ful often bklessed was his merry throat,

And thus this sweete clerk his tyme spente
And thus this sweet scholar his time spent

After his freends fyndyng and his rente.
After his friends finding and his rent.

This carpenter hadde wedded newe a wyf,
The carpenter had wedded new a wife,

Which that he lovede moore than his lyf;
Which that he loved more than his life;

Of eighteteene yeer she was of age.
Of eighteen year she was of age.

Jalous he was, and heeld hire narwe in cage,
Jealous he was, and held her narrow in cage,

For she was wylde and yong, and he was old
For she was wild and young, and he was old

And demed hymself been lik a cokewold.
And deemed himself been like a cuckold.

Fig 13 II

The English, Viking and Norman Mixture

The previous chapters have given details of all the different tribes and peoples that invaded the shores of Britain after the Romans had left, where they originally came from and what languages they spoke.

Thus far the evolution of spoken English has been in steps: firstly from the fifth century with waves of attack and the eventual occupation by the Angles, Saxons, Jutes and Frisians. Although they spoke in their various dialects of the same northern European Germanic tongue, they did adopt a few Brythonic words and phrases from the indigenous British Celts. They also adopted Latin-based words from previous associations with the Romans. These differing northern European voices, with their variances in dialect, would intermingle and create the basis of a new Germanic language, which is now referred to as Anglo-Saxon or Old English.

From the eighth century onwards the Danish and Norwegian Vikings would plunder and settle, bringing with them another version of the same Germanic language, which is now referred to as Old Norse. Together, the English and the Viking amalgamation would become the second step in establishing a spoken English and the basis for the variety of English dialects we have today.

The third step is the effect of the Norman invasion in 1066 and what followed. The Normans brought with them an eclectic mix of languages: Old Norse from the Viking element; a Germanic influence from the Franks, in the form of their northern French dialect; Flemish from the army supporting Matilda of Flanders, the wife of William; and the Brythonic-based language of the mercenary Bretons.

The Middle English melting pot that resulted laid the foundation for the English language people read today. Even so, spoken English at this time sounded very Germanic and would not be readily understood in modern times. This scenario rang true for approximately six centuries, including the Elizabethan period. It was during the time of the Stuarts when spoken English began to resemble that of our modern English.

The various Germanic invading forces would pronounce the same words differently, pronounce some letters differently and sometimes have their own characters for different letters altogether. They would also have their own local dialect words to add to the confusion. Linguistically this then leads on to the study of the different sounds of these various peoples: how these sounds are interchangeable throughout the Germanic speaking lands; the effect it had on the English language, and in particular, spoken English.

The Old English Latin alphabet, which originally contained twenty-four characters, was a dramatic change from the Anglo-Saxon futhorc runes that had been used previously, which normally consisted of thirty-three characters. The Old English alphabet had some very distinct variations, too, compared with the twenty-six letters of the English version today. Additional Anglo-Saxon sounds and letters that did not appear in the Latin alphabet had to be catered for, and extra characters were created. The Old Norse Latin alphabet had even more letters than Old English, and is still evident today in the Icelandic alphabet of thirty-two characters.

In England, the move away from the futhorc runes to a Latin-based alphabet was initiated through the teaching of the Irish missionaries who came over to convert the pagan English to Christianity. As a result, slowly but surely the Old English alphabet would become more popular during the following centuries and was gradually adopted as normal custom and practice. The Latin alphabet was the basic foundation for the construction of the Old English version. However, it did include some letters that were based on Anglo-Saxon runic characters. A total of twenty letters were exact copies from the Latin alphabet, whilst three Latin letters were altered to create two new symbols, Æ and Ð, to incorporate two sounds pronounced *ea* and *eth* respectively. Another two letters were adapted from the futhorc runes, Ƿ and Þ, the former being the forerunner of the W and the latter being the letter *thorn* representing *th* as in thorn and thin. The letters J, K, Q and Z were not used by the English in their writings

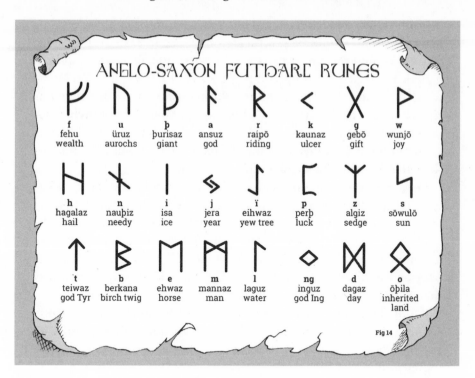

ANGLO-SAXON FUTHARC RUNES

f	**u**	**þ**	**a**	**r**	**k**	**g**	**w**
fehu	üruz	þurisaz	ansuz	raipō	kaunaz	gebō	wunjō
wealth	aurochs	giant	god	riding	ulcer	gift	joy
h	**n**	**i**	**j**	**ï**	**p**	**z**	**s**
hagalaz	nauþiz	isa	jera	eihwaz	perþ	algiz	sōwulō
hail	needy	ice	year	yew tree	luck	sedge	sun
t	**b**	**e**	**m**	**l**	**ng**	**d**	**o**
teiwaz	berkana	ehwaz	mannaz	laguz	inguz	dagaz	ōþila
god Tyr	birch twig	horse	man	water	god Ing	day	inherited land

Fig 14

Old English Alphabet

A	Ā	Æ	Ǣ	B	C	D	E	Ē	F	ȝ or G	H	I	Ī	L
a	ā	æ	ǣ	b	c	d	e	ē	f	ȝ or g	h	i	ī	l

M	N	O	Ō	P	R	S	T	Ð	U	Ū	Ƿ or W	Y	Ý
m	n	o	ō	p	r	s	t	ð	u	ū	ƿ or w	y	ý

Notes

There was not a standard alphabet and through time there were a number of alterations

The k sound in Old English was represented by c

The qu sound was represented by cw as in cwic (quick)

j and v were rarely used and were variants of i and u

Fig 15

or manuscripts and, as such, did not appear in the new alphabet. The hard 'K' sound would be represented by C, as in *castel* for a castle. This is in complete contrast to the Old Norse alphabet, which did not include the C at all and opted for the K, as in *kastali*, the Old Norse word for castle. The *qu* sound in Old English was written down as *cw*, as in *cwic* for quick. The Old Norse alphabet did not include Q, either; the J was pronounced differently and represented by the letter I; the sound of the letter Z would be incorporated into the sound of the letter X, as in the word xylophone today.

Both the Anglo-Saxons and the Vikings had many more vowel characters in their writing than there are in Modern English. Initially they had A, E, I, O and U, as in the present day, but in addition the letter Y. At this time the letter Y was purely a vowel and not made into a consonant until around 1200. There are still many examples of the Y being used as a vowel in modern English, with rhyme, hymn, dye, thyme, likely, nicely, lying and so on.

All of these six vowels would have had their own distinct vowel sounds. This same set of six vowels then formed another group with accents above them, thus making an additional six characters to represent more vowel sounds.

The Anglo-Saxons and Vikings also joined certain vowels together to create even more characters, for example Æ and Œ. By placing accents over these as well, another four vowel sounds were created. In Old Norse a forward-slanting line was also put through the O to make an Ø, and if an accent was added another two letters evolved; the Ø still exists in modern Scandinavian alphabets.

There were therefore between the Anglo-Saxons and Vikings fourteen to eighteen vowel characters representing each of their various sounds. Over the passage of time, and especially during the Middle English period, the accents over the vowels were eliminated; the joined-up letters, or ligatures, would be practically done away with, and the letter Y would become both a consonant and a vowel. (The conversion of the letter Y to a consonant will be explained later on.)

In the present day, the number of vowel sounds has remained roughly the same as in Old English, but the vast majority are now represented by the five vowel characters, the A E I O U of today, plus the letter Y. There are still a few examples where the ligatures persist, such as encyclopædia and mediæval, but these archaic usages are disappearing.

Modern Icelandic Alphabet

Letter	name	vowel or consonant	pronunciation in a word
A a	a	vowel	a as in hat
Á á	á	vowel	ow as in cow
B b	bé	consonant	same as English pronunciation
D d	dé	consonant	same as English pronunciation
Ð ð	eð (eth)	consonant	th as in farther
E e	e	vowel	e as in bed
É é	é	vowel	ye as in yes
F f	eff	consonant	same as English pronunciation
G g	ge	consonant	hard g as in garden
H h	há	consonant	hard h as in hop (not silent as in heir)
I i	i	vowel	i as in hit
Í í	í	vowel	ee as in three
J j	joð (yoth)	consonant	y as in yellow
K k	ká	consonant	same as English pronunciation
L l	ell	consonant	same as English pronunciation
M m	emm	consonant	same as English pronunciation
N n	enn	consonant	same as English pronunciation
O o	o	vowel	o as in hot
Ó ó	ó	vowel	o as in hole
P p	pé	consonant	same as English pronunciation
R r	err	consonant	rolled as in Scottish dialect
S s	ess	consonant	same as English pronunciation
T t	té	consonant	same as English pronunciation
U u	u	vowel	u as in hut
Ú ú	ú	vowel	oo as in swoon
V v	vaff	consonant	same as English pronunciation
X x	ex	consonant	cks as in locks
Y y	ufsilon y	vowel	y as in yes
Ý ý	ufsilon ý	vowel	ee as in three
Þ þ	þorn (thorn)	consonant	th as in thick
Æ æ	æ	vowel	i as in line
Ö ö	ö	vowel	i as in bird

Note C (se), Q (kú) and W (tvöfalt vaff) are used only in foreign words
Z is no longer used and was replaced with an S in 1973

Fig 16

This streamlining of the language may have been one of the reasons behind what is called the 'Great Vowel Shift'. What has happened subsequently is that each vowel character in Modern English has several pronunciations including a number of regional differences. If two of these vowels are placed together, the fluctuations in pronunciation will increase yet again, creating even more variations.

The Great Vowel Shift was a phenomenon in the English language which began in the very early 1400s and lasted for over three centuries, well after the Middle English era had finished. Historians have put forward a number of theories to explain this monumental change in spoken English without coming to a uniform conclusion or explanation. The debate continues.

Following on from streamlining the number of vowel characters was the introduction of hundreds of foreign European words into the language, which could have been a catalyst for this linguistic revolution. The shift may have been fuelled by the influence of the Norman-French spoken by royalty, aristocrats, the courts and the courtiers up to the time of Henry V; it may have been a combination of several factors. Furthermore, these vast changes to the language were adopted at different rates throughout the country with many inconsistencies and regional variations.

The pronunciation of the majority of long vowel sounds changed, and some short vowel sounds too. The vowels were now being pronounced much higher inside the mouth and further forward than before. The effect was widespread and dramatic, and to describe it as extraordinary would be a massive understatement. It would also cement strong regional differences and play a big part in the foundation of the English dialects in use today.

Middle English was, in the main, a mixture of Anglo-Saxon, Old Norse and Norman-French. Therefore the foundation of the language at the time was an eclectic concoction of pronunciations, vocabulary and grammar. This has resulted in a variety of sounds for W, U, V and F, which are interchangeable with one another not only in English but also throughout northern Europe, both then and now.

Originally the W was represented by the runic-based letter *wyn*, Ρ, before being changed to double-U and written as UU. By the fourteenth century it was common to write it as W. No other European language has a double-U sound except Welsh. The French say *double-V*, as do the Spanish and Portuguese. The Germans pronounce it quite simply as *Vee*. In Italian and Latin it doesn't appear at all, neither as double-U nor as double-V.

Old English and Old Norse Vowels

vowel	description	pronunciation
a	a soft short vowel sound	'a' as in 'human'
ā	longer version of 'a' above	'ahh' as in father
æ	a hard short vowel sound	'a' as in 'hat'
ǣ	longer version of 'æ' above	a long 'ay'
e	hard short vowel sound	'a' as in mate
ē	longer version of 'e' above	no equivalent in Modern English
i	hard short vowel	as in 'it'
ī	longer version of 'i' above pronounced 'ee'	as in 'sardine'
o	a hard short vowel	as in 'cot'
ō	a longer version of 'o' above rhyming with 'toe'	as in 'tone' but stretched
u	a hard short vowel	as in 'put'
ū	a longer version of 'u' above	as in 'nude'
y	a hard short vowel like 'u' above	rhyming with 'sue'
ȳ	a longer version of 'y' above	rhyming with whom

Additional Old Norse vowels

œ	a short vowel sound pronounced 'ir'	as in bird
œ̄	a longer version of 'œ' above	no equivalent in Modern English
Ø	a short vowel sound pronounced 'er'	rhyming with 'her'
Ǿ	a longer version of 'Ø' above	no equivalent in Modern English
Ǫ	a short vowel sound pronounced 'or'	sounds like 'or' in 'storm'
Ǭ	longer version of 'Ǫ' above	no equivalent in Modern English

Fig 17

Some examples of one vowel sound variations including the letter 'y'

A variations as found in	hat hate human father Thames path (regional variations – either parth or rhymes with hath)
E variations as found in	end even English women her here gather firemen the (pronounced 'the' before a consonant and 'thee' before a vowel – generally speaking)
I variations as found in	hit like ski lentil girl
O variations as found in	hot over oven two women conduct (c'nduct or con-duct)
U variations as found in	hut put (regional dialect 'poot') rune tune (regional dialect toon)
Y variations as found in	thyme rhythm likely martyr

Fig 18

Some examples of two vowel sound variations

ai	fair pain aisle naive said dais
au	pause laugh because
ea	beak bear bread break beard early create react ideal
ee	eel deer seer
ei	eider heir ceiling reign weir surfeit foreign
eo	theory geography creole
eu	feud
ia	dial parliament variate Anglian liar
ie	pier crier friend mien view diet alien collie fiend collier
io	trio riot lotion prior onion idiot iota ion union
oa	boar moat
oe	poet poem poetry doer
oi	toil choir reservoir
oo	book moor flood roof
ou	our your endeavour journey out would tour souvenir courage callous
ua	dual persuade truant jaguar
ue	duel rescue suede cruet duet glued
ui	fruit suite ruin build penguin
uo	duo
uu	duumvir vacuum

Fig 19

The letter U in English, apart from its varying vowel sounds as previously described, can also be pronounced as a W, as in suede, persuade, suite, queen, quick, quiet, penguin and many more.

Through the ages the letter V has been synonymous with the letter U, mainly due to the fact that in Latin the Romans did not distinguish between V the consonant and U the vowel – they used the same symbol for both. At one period of time, including the reign of the Stuarts, it was correct to put a V at the beginning of a word such as *vpon*, for upon, but as a U if it was not the initial letter, as in lute.

In Old English the letter V could also be pronounced softly and sound more like an F. In German today the V is pronounced two ways: as an F in *volk* (pronounced *folk*) and as a V in *verboten*.

The letter W in German today is pronounced as a V, with *west* being pronounced as *vest*.

The letter F in Old English was also said in various ways: it was said as a hard F and sounded like a V, but also as a soft F and pronounced as a W. This transference of sounds can readily be seen in the Old English word for hawk, *hafoc*, which also appears in place names such as *Hafoc cirice* and *Hafoc burh*. The F was pronounced softly and as a result was replaced with a U and recorded in the Domesday Book in 1086 as *Hauekchierch* and *Hauochesberie*. At a later date the U was changed to a W and, with slight changes in the spellings, became Hawkchurch and Hawkesbury in Devon and South Gloucestershire respectively.

This transference has occurred numerous times with other words, place names and surnames. Erwarton, Suffolk, derives from a farmstead *(tun)* belonging to *Eoforwaerd*, a nickname given to a brave warrior, *boar guard*. The village was recorded in 1196 as *Euerewardeston*, with the W eventually replacing the U and abbreviated to Erwarton.

A good number of English surnames derived from Old English warrior nicknames pertaining to the wolf, such as *wulf mœr* ('wolf famous'), *wulf sige* ('wolf victory') and *wulf nōth* ('wolf boldness'), and many more. Invariably the F was pronounced softly and at a later date was replaced with a U or W, and eventually dropped altogether. Names would evolve like Woolmer (*wulf mœr*), Wolsey (*wulf sige*) and Woolner or Woolnough (*wulf nōth*). Occasionally W at the beginning of *wulf* was so soft that it became superfluous and was omitted, creating the Old Norse-based surnames Ulf and Ulph.

There has never been an official body, either from Parliament or by royal decree, dictating a standardised English. It has been left

to develop with many contradictions and the W, U, V and F letters became so interchangeable that inconsistencies have arisen.

The word 'of' is pronounced as *ov,* but add another F and it changes to 'off'. However, in the phrase, 'I will have to', the word 'have' is usually pronounced *haff,* but in 'I have done that', it is pronounced as *hav.*

The initial letter of the word *vin* was pronounced with a soft V and subsequently substituted by the letter W to produce the English word wine. Yet in the word 'vineyard', pronounced *vinyard,* where grapes are grown, the pronunciation of the letter V has continued.

From the borrowed Latin word *vermis,* the initial letter was commonly pronounced softly by the English who changed it to *wyrm,* meaning 'worm'. However, if a book is eaten by bookworms, it has been vermiculated, and vermicide is used to kill them.

The interchangeability and inconsistency of W, U, V and F has also thrown up even more oddities. In the Domesday Book a Norfolk village was recorded as *Stiuekai* (pronounced *stewkey).* The U was also pronounced with a harder F and the settlement became known as Stiffkey, though it was still referred to as *Stewkey* by some of the locals; both versions are shown on the village sign.

The word 'lieu' is ordinarily pronounced as *lew,* but if the U has the F sound it becomes *lief* or *lewf.* With the suffix *-tenant* being added to the word, *lefftenant* evolves but still keeps the lieutenant spelling.

Perhaps the most consistent inconsistencies are pronunciations of numerous places ending in *-wich* or *-wick.* The spelling of the suffixes has remained the same with the pronunciation of the W, as in Aldwich, Nantwich and Prestwick. Many, however, have the softer U sound and the W becomes defunct although still present in the spelling, as in Berwick, Keswick and Warwick, pronounced *Berrick, Kezick* and *Worrick.*

The W, U, V and F sounds are still interchangeable throughout northern Europe. By adding an -e onto the end of suit it changes the U sound to a W and alters the pronunciation to *sweet* (suite). A northern European will pronounce it as either *sfeet* or *sveet,* dependent on where they originate. Many more examples could be given.

Between them, all the invading forces that came over and settled had different sounds for the letter G. There were four main distinct pronunciations, which still exist today in one form or another. Firstly,

the hard G, as in 'gate'; secondly as a softer sounding J, as in 'gaol' (jail); thirdly a Ch, as in the pronunciation of 'loch', though the Ch generally hardened up to a K sound later on; fourthly the very soft G, sounding as a Y as in *regn* and pronounced *rayen*, later to become the English word 'rain'.

What has clouded the issue somewhat is the fact that all these sounds were written down as a G. The letter Y was still only used as a vowel, in words such as *cyder*. It was not until the late twelfth and early thirteenth century when words spelt with a G but pronounced as a Y actually had their spelling changed to the Y. But this process was ad hoc and not officially enforced, and it would appear that the scribes of the day were halfway through this mammoth task and downed tools realising that some people were still using the other pronunciation. This resulted in many words in the English language containing a G with a Y pronunciation. This inconsistency of the letter G will be shown in the next few paragraphs.

The Wuffings, the ruling hierarchy of East Anglia, were linked with the royal dynasty in southern Sweden and invited over by the East Angles to settle and rule. The majority of Swedes today pronounce the city of Gothenberg as *Yowterbury*; and the Swedish ex-England football manager, Sven Goran Eriksson, pronounced his middle name as *Yorran*. In Denmark the town of Skagen is pronounced *Skayen* and the Danish female Christian name of Solvejg is pronounced *Solvaye*.

Guernsey, a British Crown dependency, historically was a Viking outpost after the invasion of the Norsemen in AD 911 and a staging post for the Conquest in 1066. The older *Guernésiais* generation today, speaking in their local dialect, still pronounce the island in the Norman-Viking way as *Yernsey* and refer to themselves as *Yernesiais* or *Yernesiaise*.

In North Yorkshire the village of Chop Gate is pronounced *Chop Yatt*, and in some northern counties of England the dialect word for style is *stiggle*, which is reflected in the surnames of Styles and Stiggals.

The English surnames Gates and Yates have the same derivation, either a 'dweller by a gate' or a 'gatekeeper', from the Old English word *geat*. Both surnames are fairly widespread, but the highest density of Gates is found south of London and the epicentre for Yates is north-west England. This regional difference perhaps would tie in with the Saxon strongholds in the south and the Angle and Viking strongholds in the north.

Examples of some Old English words and place names containing g pronounced as y and replaced with y or i

Old English	Pronunciation	Modern English
byrg	burry	bury
dræg	dray	dray
éage	eye	eye
fægen	fayen	fain
fæger	fayer	fair (bright, fine)
gánian	yaarnian	yawn
Géapum	Yearpum	Yapham (Yorkshire)
Geard cyln	Yeard kiln	Yarkhill (Herefordshire)
géar	yeear	year
geard	yeard	yard (enclosure)
gearn	yearn	yarn (thread)
Geoc ham	Yeoke ham	(y)Ickham (Kent)
geoguth	yeoy'th	youth
Géol	Yeaol	Yule(tide)
geolu	yeolu	yellow
geon	yeon	yon
geong	yeong	young
geongmann	yeongman	youngman (yeoman)
georn	yeorn	yearn
geostran dæg	yeastran day	yesterday
gése	yease	yes
gield	yaeld	yield
gierd	yeard	yard (a measure)
Gipeswic	Yippeswich	(y)Ipswich (Suffolk)
gist	yist	yeast
Gœhdun	Yeahdun	Yeadon (Yorkshire)
grighund	greyhund	greyhound
Gyrdleah	Yerdleah	Yardley (several places)
hægl	hayel	hail
hegwagen	heywayen	haywain
pægel	payel	pail
regn	rayen	rain
sælig	seely	silly
stæger	steeyer	stair
stig	sty	sty
stigel	styel	stile
tægel	tayel	tail
twéntig	twenty	twenty
ðritig	threrty	thirty
Wódnesdæg	Wodensday	Wednesday

Fig 20

Some Modern English words containing letter g with y pronunciation

Origin	Middle English spelling	Modern spelling
Old English beorht	bryht, briht, brict	bright
Old French degnier	deine, deigne, daigne	deign
Old English æhta	eighte, eghte, aghte	eight
Old French enseigne	ensigne, enseyne	ensign
Old French feigne	feigne, fein	feign
Old English feohte	fiht(e), feht(e), fyghte (over 20 variations)	fight
Old English flyht	fliht, flygte, flyghte	flight
Old English fryhto	friʒt, fryʒt, freyte	fright
Old French forein	forein, foreyn,	foreign
Old English hēhthu	heyghte, heyth	height
Old English hēah	hegh, heigh, hi (over 20 variations)	high
Old English cniht	cnigt, cnicht, cnict knict, knight (over 40 variations)	knight
Old English liht	liht, liʒt, lighte	light
Old English mihtig	mihti, myʒty	mighty
Old English nǣgan	neyghe, neigh	neigh
Old English nǣgebúr	negebur, neyghebour	neighbour
Old English nǣh	neʒh, neghe, nyhe, nighe	nigh
Old English niht	niʒte, nyght, nyghte	night
Old English plihtan	pliht, pliʒt, plyʒht	plight
Old French poignant	poynaunt, poignant	poignant
Old French reigne	reigne, reign	reign
Old French reigner	resygn, resygne	resign
Old English riht	riht, rihte, ryʒt, righte (over 20 variations)	right

Fig 21 |

94

Some Modern English words containing letter g with y pronunciation

Origin	Middle English spelling	Modern spelling
Old English siht	syhte, syght, syghte	sight
OE segn, OF seign	signe, segne	sign
Old Norse slēttr	sleght, sliht, slight	slight
Old English þēoh	thei, thegh, thighe	thigh
Old English wegan	weien, weighen, weigh	weigh
Old Norse weht Old English wiht	weiht, weght, weight (over 20 variations)	weight

There were many differences in the spelling of words in Old English, Old Norse, Old French and Middle English.

English was written phonetically and therefore many variations. Standards in spelling came many centuries later.

Fig 21 II

The G was also pronounced as a hard K, evident in vernacular English with the pronunciation of words such as *anythink, somethink* and *nothink,* and also in the place name Cogenhoe, Northamptonshire, pronounced *Cook'noe.*

Putting an N in front of a G would ordinarily create the sound similar in Standard English to verbs ending in *-ing.* But once again inconsistencies arise, especially on a regional basis. Verbs such as hunting, shooting and fishing in Standard English will have the *-ing* sound. However, the West Country will pronounce them as *hunten, shooten* and *fishen,* whilst in East Anglia as *hunt'n, shoot'n* and *fish'n.* London and surrounding counties however will say *huntin', shootin'* and *fishin',* whereas the North and the Midlands will pronounce the G as in *huntinga, shootinga* and *fishinga.*

The mixture of all the incoming dialects and languages, from the Angles and Saxons to the Vikings and Normans and subsequent Plantagenets, also led to an interchange of the way Gu and the W were pronounced. As previously described, the G can be pronounced softly,

DISTRIBUTION
OF SURNAME
EATES
1881AD census

Map 11

DISTRIBUTION
OF SURNAME
YATES
1881AD census

Map 12

sounding like *ya*. If this is followed by the U being pronounced as a W, the combination would sound similar to *y'wa*. This tended to be based on Norman-French pronunciation. The initial *y* would become superfluous and silent and was eventually omitted, leaving the W as the initial sound. But the Plantagenets from central France pronounced the G as the hard G with the sound of the U becoming so soft it was omitted. There are a few examples today, however, where the U is pronounced as a W after the G, for example 'sanguine', 'language' and 'penguin'.

Generally speaking, common usage determined which way a word was pronounced – whichever became predominant tended to become the accepted norm, either as a G or a W. However, a few words have evolved alongside one another with both pronunciations but similar meanings.

The variances of pronouncing the letters O, U and G have produced even more variations when those letters are put alongside one another in words containing *ough*. There are nine different distinct sounds in Standard English for *ough*; it can even be argued there is a tenth form if the word *hiccough* (hiccup) is included, a late sixteenth-century onomatopoeic word for an involuntary spasm.

Examples of words with either Gu or W initial letters with similar meaning

Gu	W
guarantee	warranty
guard	ward
guardian	warden
guardrobe	wardrobe
guerre	war
guerrilla*	warrior
guile	wile
Guillaum	William
Guyatt	Wyatt

* pronunciation gareeya

Fig 22

Regional dialects will increase the varying pronunciations even more. Standard English and southern dialects will pronounce the word 'nought' as *nort*. However, other more northern dialects range from *nart*, *nowt* and *note*: 'It's nowt t' do wi' me!' Likewise the word 'ought' will be treated in the same manner.

East Anglian dialects will say *enow* instead of *enuff* for 'enough', which in earlier times would have had a more widespread usage; in the dictionary the word *enow* is described as an archaic way of saying 'enough', as used by Shakespeare.

Words containing *augh* tend to be more consistent. There are still some variations, such as 'caught' and 'taught', with the *augh* being pronounced as *or*, but the word 'laugh' has the *augh* being pronounced *ar*, with the northern and Midland variation of *laff*.

The letter C had three different pronunciations: soft C, as in 'cell'; Ch, as in 'cello'; and a hard sound, as in 'canal'. The Vikings however did not have a C in their alphabet and used S for soft C and K for the harder sound. The latter can be seen in words like *kálfr* (calf) and *kaldr* (cold), and even today in the words *konflikt* (conflict) and *kontakt* (contact).

Examples of some words containing 'ough' and their varying pronunciations

ow (as in cow)	off	o (as in go)	ock	och	uff	oo	uh	or	up
bough	cough	although	hough	lough	chough	through	borough	bought	hiccough
doughty	trough	dough			clough		thorough	brought	
drought		furlough			enough			fought	
plough		though			rough			nought	
slough					tough			ought	
sough								sought	
enough*								thought	
nought*								wrought	
ought*									

* Regional variations

Fig 23

The cartoon below is based on a regional BBC radio presenter advocating that the English language should be made more simple... and that instead of the ten variations of pronouncing 'ough'... that there should be just the one uniform pronunciation of 'ow'... it would make the English language easier for young people to learn as well as for foreigners.

During the Middle English period the letter H was now being used to characterise and separate various sounds, such as alongside the C to distinguish the Ch-sounding C from the soft and hard C. This process evolved quite organically, resulting in many inconsistencies still evident in Modern English today. The word 'chapel' evolves from the Norman-French word *capele*, and is typically pronounced *chapel* by the English. However, sometimes it was pronounced in the same way as in the Norman-French, as seen in villages containing the name Capel.

The influence of Norman-French on the Old English root word *candel* is another example. Although called a candle, the candle maker was called a chandler and a holder for a number of candles is called a chandelier, but a portable holder for a candle is called a candlestick. A further example of differing pronunciations is that both 'canal' and 'channel' derive from the Norman-French root word *canel*. So that's the root canal work done.

To add to the confusion, the inconsistencies prevailed throughout the evolution of English when words containing Ch were pronounced as a K and the role of the H was ignored, as in 'mechanic', 'Christmas' and 'technical'. To make matters worse, adopted foreign words with Ch would not be anglicised and would keep their foreign sound, which resulted in the Ch being pronounced as a Sh, as in 'chevron' and 'chivalry'.

To confuse the situation even further, especially during the height of the English Renaissance, some adopted Italian words containing the letter C were not converted and still retain the Ch sound, as in 'cello' and 'concerto' – both of which can be heard in a concert (*konsert*).

In Old English, the Ch sound of C changed when placed after an S to a Sh sound. The Vikings used K instead of C, and pronounced it as Sk. For example, fish was spelled *fisc* in Old English and *fisk* in Old Norse.

The two runic-based letters eth (Ð, ð) and thorn (Þ, þ) represented the sounds of a soft Th and a hard Th, as in 'broth' (soft Th) and 'father' (hard Th). Their grammatical usage was not strictly adhered to and was dependent on where they appeared in the particular word, and in which context. These two letters are still used in Icelandic text, with the thorn being used at the beginning of the word and the eth within the word, as in *Hvað segir þu?*, which translates as 'How are you?'

The eth, both upper case and lower case (Ð and ð), was used during the Middle English period less frequently up until around 1300, when it practically became defunct. It was replaced with a new combination

Some examples of the variations of the letter C from Old English, Old Norse and Norman-French into English pronunciations today

English words today	Old English	Old Norse	Norman French
cake	-	kaka	-
candle, chandelier chandler, candlestick	candel	-	caundele
castle	castel	kastali	castel
canal channel	-	-	canel
cell	-	-	cella
chapel, Capel (place names)	-	-	capele
child	cild	-	-
church kirk	cirice	kirkja	-
cleave	clēofan	kljūfa	-
clothe	clāð	klaeða	-
cross	cros	kross	croix
cull kill	cyllan	-	-
merchant mercantile Mercer (surname)	-	-	mercer

Examples of some modern Danish words including a k with English equivalent c or ch

kat *cat* • **kable** *cable* • **kabine** *cabin* • **kaffe** *coffee* • **kage** *cake* • **kalender** *calendar* • **kaliber** *calibre* • **kalif** *caliph* • **kalorie** *calorie* • **kalv** *calf* • **kam** *comb* • **kamille** *hamomile* • **kampagne** *campaign* • **kanal** *channel* • **kannibal** *cannibal* • **kano** *canoe* • **kanon** *canon* • **kantine** *canteen* • **kaos** *chaos* • **kapacitet** *capacity* • **kapel** *chapel* • **kapital** *capital* • **kappe** *cap* • **kapsel** *capsule* • **kaptajn** *captain* • **karakter** *character* • **karamel** *caramel* • **kardinal** *cardinal* • **karotte** *carrot* • **karrusel** *carousel* • **kartografi** *cartography* • **karton** *carton* • **kaste** *cast* • **katapult** *catapult* • **katedral** *cathedral* • **kategori** *category* • **kavaleri** *cavalry* • **kerub** *cherub* • **Kina** *China* • **klar** *clear* • **klasse** *class* • **klassisk** *classic* • **klinisk** *clinic* • **klovn** *clown* • **kløver** *clover* • **klub** *club* • **klubhus** *clubhouse* • **kniv** *knife* • **knop** *knob* • **ko** *cow* • **kobber** *copper* • **kode** *code* • **koffein** *caffeine* • **kogebog** *cookbook* • **kogt** *cooked* • **kok** *cook* • **kold** *cold* • **koldblodit** *coldblooded* • **kollega** *colleague* • **kollidere** *collide* • **koloni** *colony* • **kombination** *combination* • **komedie** *comedy* • **komet** *comet* • **komfort** *comfort* • **komma** *comma* • **komme** *come* • **kommentar** *comment* • **kommerciel** *commercial* • **kommission** *commission* • **kompas** *compass* • **kompleks** *complex* • **kondom** *condom* • **konference** *conference* • **konfetti** *confetti* • **konflikt** *conflict* • **konkret** *concrete* • **konservativ** *conservative* • **konsistent** *consistent* • **konsonant** *consonant* • **kop** *cup* • **kopi** *copy* • **kor** *choir* • **koral** *coral* • **korrekt** *correct* • **krabbe** *crab* • **krampe** *cramp* • **krater** *crater* • **krise** *crisis* • **Kristen** *Christian* • **kritiker** *critic* • **krone** *crown*

Fig 24

Examples of Old English words with sc in the spelling being linked with Old Norse (Viking) including present day

Old English words	English words from Anglo-Saxon pronunciations	English words from Viking pronunciations	linked Scandinavian words today
fisc	fish	Fisk (surname)	fisk
sceab	-	scab	-
scead	shade	-	skygge
sceap	shape	(land)scape	(land)scab
sceot	shot	-	skotte
scinn	-	skin	-
scipe	ship	skip	skib
		skipper	skipper
scipwræc	shipwreck	-	skibbrud
scolu	shoal	school	skole
scoru	-	score	-
screpan	-	scrape	skrabe
scriccettan	shriek	screech	skrig
		skrike (Yorks dialect)	
scrybb	shrub	scrub	-
scyrte	shirt	skirt	skjorte
scytel	shuttle	scuttle	-

Examples of some English words with sh derived from Old English sc

shad	*sceadd*	shade	*sceadu*	shadow	*sceadwe*	shaft	*sceaft*
shag	*sceacga*	shake	*sceacan*	shall	*sceal*	shambles	*scamel*
shame	*scamu*	shank	*scanca*	shape	*scieppan*	shard	*sceard*
share	*scear*	sharp	*scearp*	shave	*sceafan*	sheaf	*scēaf*
shear	*sceran*	sheath	*sceað*	shed	*scēad*	sheen	*scēne*
sheep	*scēap*	sheet	*scēte*	shelf	*scylf*	shell	*scēll*
shepherd	*scēaphirde*	sheriff	*scīrgerefa*	shield	*sceld*	shift	*sciftan*
shilling	*scilling*	shimmer	*scimerian*	shin	*scinu*	shine	*scīnan*

Fig 25

Examples of some English words with sh derived from Old English sc

ship	*scip*	shire	*scīr*	shiver	*scifre*	shoal	*scolu*
shoe	*scōh*	shoot	*scēotan*	shop	*sceoppa*	short	*sceort*
shove	*scūfan*	shovel	*scofl*	show	*sceawian*	shower	*scūr*
shred	*scrēade*	shrew	*scrēawa*	shrift	*scrīfan*	shrike	*scric*
shrine	*scrin*	shrink	*scrincan*	shroud	*scrūd*	shrub	*scrybb*
shun	*scunnian*	shut	*scyttan*	shuttle	*scytel*	shy	*scēoh*

Some examples showing sh / sk historical link in modern English and Scandinavian words

ash aske	*ashamed* skamfuld	*ashen* askegrå	*ash tree* aske træ
bishop biskop	*bush* busk	*bushy* buskede	*Danish* Dansk
devilish djævelsk	*English* Engelsk	*Finnish* Finske	*Flemish* Flamske
fresh frisk	*freshness* friskhed	*mash* maske	*marsh* marsk
ploughshare plovskær	*Polish* Polske	*Scottish* Skoteske	*shall* skall
shallot skalotteløg	*shalt* skal du	*sharp* skarp	*sheer* ren og skær
shield skjold	*shin* skinneben	*shine* skinne	*shiny* skinnende
shoe sko *shoe horn* sko horn	*shoe leather* sko læder	*shoemaker* skomager	
shod skoet	*shone* skinnede	*shoot* skyde	*shot* skotte
shoulder skulder *shovel* skovl	*shovel* board skovl bord	*shrine* skrin	
shrank skrumpede	*shrug* skuldertræk	*shrunk* skrumpet	*Spanish* Spanske
sunshine solskin	*Swedish* Svensk	*thrush* trøske	*wash* vask
washed vasket *washing machine* vaskemaskine	*wish* ønske	*wishing* ønsker	

Fig 25 II

of two letters. The letter H was now taking on another role and being used after a T to create a relatively new character for the Th sound.

The thorn (Þ and þ) lasted a little longer but gradually petered out by the time of the new printing presses in the late 1400s and early 1500s. It had been replaced with both the new Th combination and, in a very few cases, by a flat-looking Y. The printers at the time thought the latter was so similar to a Y that they used the Y instead. This gave rise to the word 'the' being printed as *ye*, but at the time was still pronounced as *the* or *thee*, dependent on what word followed it. Through time, however, 'ye' was incorrectly pronounced as *yee*, as in *Ye Olde Tuck Shoppe*, and was confused with the pronunciation of 'ye', being the second person plural of you and sometimes its singular, as in 'Where are ye?'

The eth (Ð and ð) was also very much misrepresented during this period, and on many occasions was mistaken for the letter D, which is quite understandable when looking at both the upper case Ð and lower case ð. Many words, names and places today contain the letters D or d instead of the converted Ð or ð, as in Hadfield (*hað feld*, 'heath field') in Derbyshire, and Sudborough (*suð burh*, 'south borough') in Lincolnshire. The surname Gooderam and its various alternatives derive from *Guð ormr*, originally pronounced *Guthoram*, being an Old Norse Viking warrior nickname for a battle snake.

The letter H has had a very chequered life throughout the history of written and spoken English. In Old Norse and Old English it was pronounced very hard and strong. The H was also used more regularly as an initial letter than it is today, even before a consonant and not just a vowel. However, during the Middle English period, the letter H as an initial letter became silent and practically defunct. What generally happened is that the strong sound of the letter H disappeared completely from words when followed by a vowel. It has been suggested this occurred because of the non-pronunciation of the letter H by the Normans with their particular Viking-French mix, which is still evident in the modern French pronunciation of hospital and hotel with a silent h as *'opital* and *'otel*. Invariably, the letter H was still kept in the spelling although not pronounced, as heard in the London dialects today, especially the East London Cockney accent, when they say for example, *'orse*, *'ouse* and *'ome*, for horse, house and home. But the H did make some sort of a comeback during the reign of the Stuarts, to be explained later.

Examples of letter H as strongly pronounced initial letter

hlædan - to load	hlædel - ladle	hlæden - bucket
hlæder - ladder	hlædrede - steps	hlæderstæf – ladder staff (rung of a ladder)
hlæne – lean	hlænnes - leanness	hlænian - make lean (to starve)
hláf - loaf	hláfæta - loaf eater	hláfwæte – loaf wheat (bread wheat)
hleahtor - laughter	hleahtrian - deride (make laughter of)	hleahtorsmið – laughter smith (laughter maker)
hléapan - leap	hléapere - leaper (dancer)	hléapestre - female leaper (female dancer)
hlid - lid	hlidgeat - lidgate	hlidod - lidded (having a lid)
hlystan - listen	hlysting - listening	hlystnere - listener
hnappian - nap (sleep)	hnappod - napped (slept)	hnappung - napping (sleeping)
hnutu - nut	hnutbéam - nut tree	hnutcyrnel - kernel
hréaw – raw	hréawan – to be raw	hréawnes – rawness
hriddel – riddle (to sort)	hridder – ridder (sieve)	hridrian – ridden (to sift)
hrímforst – rime frost	hrímgicel – icicle	hrímig – rimy, frosty
hring – ring	hringfinger - ring finger	hringgeat - ring gate
hróf - roof	hróftigel - roof tile	hróftimber - roof timber
hrycg - ridge	hrycgweg - ridge way	hrycgbán – ridge bone (spine)

Fig 26

Some examples of Old English words with hw and Old Norse with hv as initial letters being transposed, and w becoming the dominant sound

hwæl *whale* · hwearf *wharf* · hwæt *what* · hwǣt *wheat* · hwī *why* · hwēol *wheel* · hvæsa [ON] *wheeze* · hwlca *whelk* · hwelian *whelm* · hwelp *whelp* · hwanne *when* · hwanon *whence* · hwǣr *where* · hwettan *whet* · hwæðer *whether* · hwǣg *whey* · hwilc *which* · hwīl *while* · hvima [ON] *whim* · hwīnan *whine* · hwinsian *whinge* · hvirfla [ON] *whirl* · hvisk [poss ON] *whisk* · hwisprian *whisper* · hwistlian *whistle* · hwīt *white* · hwiðer *whither* · ðwītan *whittle*

Notes:
Whore - still has dominant h as it derives from OE hōre
Whooping - originates from Norman-French houper – to shout
Who - derives from OE hwā but still maintains the dominant h even though the initial letters have been transposed. This also applies to all its derivatives, whoever, whom, whomever, whomsoever, whose and whosesoever. There is no reason why, and an example of inconsistency.

Fig 27

Where H preceded a consonant it disappeared completely, both in spelling and pronunciation, as seen in fig 26. However, when H preceded the letter W, a different path was usually followed. Although the sound of the H was dropped, the letter was kept but transferred to second place and the W then preceded the H.

This change was not altogether universal, and there were some regional differences. Whilst the letter itself was transferred in the spelling, the sound was not. There are still certain dialects today that maintain a soft H sound preceding the W, especially in Scotland, the Republic of Ireland and Northern Ireland. The pronunciation of when, where and what will invariably sound somewhat similar to *hwen*, *hwere* and *hwat*, but 'who', 'whose' and 'whom' are exceptions, and H remained dominant and W became silent.

Not all was lost for the letter H. It reinvented itself during the Middle English period as well as making a comeback at a later date. It was to take on a new role and represent three distinctive sounds. Perhaps it was a sign of the times, and an indication of the language gradually moving from Middle English to a more modern version.

The H was placed after a C to represent a Ch sound to try and lessen the confusion surrounding the letter C. This only succeeded in increasing the variables and differences. It was also placed after the letter S to represent a Sh sound instead of the Anglo-Saxon Sh sound hitherto being represented by Sc.

The H also succeeded the letter T to represent both the Th sounds, as in 'mother' and 'broth', replacing the Old English letters, eth (Ð and ð) and thorn (Þ and þ).

The Old English letter called a *yogh* originally represented a Ch type sound, as in the Scottish pronunciation of 'loch' and the similar sound as in 'Bach'. It looked somewhat similar to the number three, ʒ upper case and ʒ lower case. The Normans did not care too much for runic-based letters and gradually they replaced the ʒ, usually with a G or Gh and sometimes a J or a Y.

Written English was changing with the times just as the spoken word was, but with no uniform pattern. Old English and Old Norse manuscripts and writings were generally phonetic and reflected the way words were spoken.

This principle would not alter during the Middle English period. Generally speaking, apart from the H, there was not one letter that remained silent, which is quite different from the English of today, for example in 'lamb', 'gnat' and 'know'. All letters had a purpose, a reason and a sound in Middle English.

The Normans had a very strong northern French dialect, heavily influenced by the Viking settlers from 905 and the Germanic Franks prior to that. This mix was reflected in the words they introduced, which were by and large very different to standard French.

The English language would change in its written form quite dramatically, sometimes suddenly and sometimes very gradually. Despite the changes, the language would in general still keep its Anglo-Saxon structure. Scribes and scholars were responding to the Great Vowel Shift and rewriting English phonetically to correspond with the spoken word.

The Old English scribes very rarely used K, J, Z or Q, except perhaps only when copying foreign manuscripts. The Normans introduced roughly 10,000 words into the vocabulary, some of which would include these new letters.

The Norman Qu was pronounced as a K sound followed by a W sound, replacing the equivalent Cw in Old English. Eventually, words like 'queen', 'quell' and 'quick' would replace *cwén*, *cwellan* and *cwic*.

The letter K was introduced and invariably replaced the harder-sounding C to help distinguish it from the softer-sounding C. This substitution is evident in words such as 'knight' for *cniht*, and 'knap' for *cnæpp*. At this point in time, the K was being pronounced when it preceded an N. The word 'knight' would have sounded somewhat similar to *kernycht*. The sounding of the K is still the case in the Netherlands today, where they pronounce words like *k'nei* for 'knee' and *k'napzak* for 'knapsack'. Using the K to replace the harder C was not confined just to Old English: it can also be seen in Norman-French words like *clerc* for a clergyman or scholar being replaced with clerk.

The letters J and I were regularly swapped around, and a word like *wijf* would be an alternative way of spelling *wif* (wife). The J was often used in the judicial system, as in 'judge', 'jury', 'just' and 'justice'. It was also used in ecclesiastical manuscripts when translating the Hebrew, Greek and Latin and recording names like Jerusalem and Jericho.

The letter Ú started to be phased out in the thirteenth century and was replaced by *ou*, as in *hous* for *hús* (house), and *bour* for *búr* (bower).

There was also a tendency at this time to replace the letter U with an O when it was next to the letters V, N or M. This would help make a greater visual distinction between the letters, but the O would still maintain the U's pronunciation. This can readily be seen in Modern English spellings like 'mother' and 'month' (O being pronounced as U next to an M), and the same in 'oven' (O being pronounced as U next to a V). Similar principles apply to 'come', 'love' and 'son'.

The double E and double O would make a debut during this period, replacing the letters É and Ó respectively. The long vowel sounds as in *bóc* would be written as 'booc', eventually having the hard C replaced with a K to become 'book'. The Norman-French word *se* for the area overseen by a bishop was elongated to 'see'.

Another area of change was altering words containing *ei* to either *ai* or *ay*. The Old English *weg* had been rewritten as *wei* to demonstrate the soft G sound. This was later changed in the late thirteenth century to 'way'. Similarly, *dæg* became *dei* and eventually 'day'. However, *regn* went from *rein* to 'rain' as *tægel* become *teil* and then 'tail'. This process did not happen, however, if the *ei* was before a *gh*, and words like 'eight', 'height' and 'weight' maintained the *ei* and were not altered.

As demonstrated, many significant changes of pronunciations occurred in Middle English and subsequently the spellings were altered to correspond. English was starting to evolve into the language we are more familiar with today.

Although English was originally thought to be the language of the peasants and relegated to third place by the Norman kings and the succeeding Plantagenets, it was about to make a breakthrough. It was in many ways inevitable: English was still spoken by a very large majority of the English people, whereas Norman-French was spoken by royalty and those who surrounded them, and Latin was spoken in the Church and the very exclusive education system, limited to aristocracy and royalty.

This breakthrough of the English language was a coming together of several occurrences, which perhaps started with King John in 1202 losing the possession of Normandy to Philip II of France.

After the loss of Normandy, a series of wars with France would then rage off and on for the next 300 years, including the Hundred Years' War from 1337 to 1453. This meant that throughout society, from the most humble peasant to the king himself, France was seen as the enemy. Everything that was allied to the French was seen as consorting with the enemy, including the use of Norman-French in English royal circles.

Whilst this anti-French feeling was gathering momentum, Geoffrey Chaucer, along with some of his literary contemporaries, was playing a major role in the shaping of the language. His brilliant writing, in wonderfully expressive prose, helped improve the attitude towards the English language. The time was right for English to be readily accepted by royalty and at court. English took such a hold that not only did the kings of England drop Norman-French altogether but the powerful spoke in English and conducted their affairs in English.

Another big contribution to the English-language breakthrough was that by 1385 English was being used in schools. Latin would continue to be taught as it was still considered to be the language of scholarship even though it had become a dead language in common speech. Most other subjects at school were being taught in English. It had become the principal language of the education system.

The plague in 1348/1349 and the four epidemics in the next fifty years also played an important part in promoting the English language. Proportionally there were more deaths during the outbreaks of the plague among the Norman-French-speaking ruling classes than

the English. Many of those who did survive, left and returned to their country of origin. It is estimated that the plague killed half the population of England.

The English language was now firmly on the map. Its resilience had never wavered, despite the Norman and Plantagenet efforts to relegate it into insignificance. English would grow from strength to strength and take another step forward during the reigns of the Tudors and Stuarts, especially during the Elizabethan era, the age of Shakespeare, and later still with King James I.

English had started off as a collection of regional dialects of a few Germanic tribes who had conquered and occupied parts of Britain. By the end of the Middle English period, English had become the main language of a major European country. In time, it would be extended throughout the world.

8

The Tudors

During the time of the Tudors (1485–1603), even more dramatic changes would occur in both written and spoken English. The Great Vowel Shift was still helping to reshape the pronunciation of English and the way it sounded. A number of other influences would ensure that the language would continue to develop. This particular period is recognised as the start of Early Modern English, and whilst it begins to look similar to Modern English in written form, it was still very different when spoken. Chancery Standard was still being used by royalty, government officials and bureaucrats, but there were still too many location-dependent variations to be able to describe it as a 'standard' English. The ordinary folk would still be talking in their regional dialects.

The education system under Henry VII and the first part of Henry VIII's reign became more central and expanded significantly – more so than at any time before. It was exclusive to boys. Previously, only a few boys had gone to school and they tended to come from the rich and wealthy strata in society who could afford to pay the school fees. A wider selection of boys from varying backgrounds were now included, being taught the rudiments of education. However, even then the vast majority of boys were not able to attend school as they had to go out to work. This non-attendance at school meant that they would not be taught Chancery English and their regional dialects would be maintained. This scenario existed until the Victorian age when the education system was radically reformed to include all children.

The education system in early Tudor times was harsh. Boys started school at the age of four and received a fundamental education until the age of six. These schools were called petty schools and the boys were taught to read and write, mainly in English. It is believed that 'petty' derives from the French word for small, *petit,* pronounced *pettee.* The teacher would normally be the local clergyman and the boys would spend hours writing in ink and making numerous copies of the alphabet and the Lord's Prayer. At this time the alphabet consisted of twenty-four letters, as the U and V were considered to be the same, as were the I and the J.

Some of the petty schools were also known as dame schools because they were run by women who had been lucky enough to have received some form of education.

At the age of seven some boys then went on to grammar school, where they were taught English, most probably Chancery English, along with Latin, Greek, arithmetic and the Catechism, which was a summary of questions and answers pertaining to the Christian religion in the Roman Catholic Church.

The school day at grammar schools commenced at seven o'clock in the morning during winter and six o'clock in the summer and ended at five o'clock in the afternoon. Attendance from Monday to Saturday inclusive was expected, as well as going to church on the Sunday. A school day at the petty schools was shorter to allow some of the boys to go out to work.

Discipline was excruciatingly severe. Boys were chastised with a birch stick, sometimes receiving up to fifty strokes. The much richer boys did not mind the chastisement because they could afford to pay for a whipping boy who would take their punishment instead.

The extremely rich and wealthy families tended to pay for a tutor to teach both their sons and their daughters at home. Normally girls did not have any formal education but they were expected to help with household chores, and as soon as they were able, were sent out to work to help supplement the family finances. Any education they may have received was usually second-hand from their brothers, teaching them to read and perhaps write.

During the years from 1536 to 1541 the number of schools was radically reduced following the Dissolution of the Monasteries and the closing of some monastic schools. Later Henry reinstated many of these schools and they came to be known as King's Schools or Royal Grammar Schools, some of which have survived to the present day.

The promoting of education continued during the reign of Edward VI, and a number of free grammar schools were established throughout the country for non-fee-paying pupils. These were known as King Edward VI Grammar Schools.

During Elizabeth's reign it would appear that things started to change for the better. Some girls were now allowed to attend the petty schools or the dame schools, but they were not yet allowed to have a grammar school education nor attend university.

The printing press had a remarkable effect on the written word and, eventually, the spoken word. It became one of the main catalysts in creating a modern Standard English that is recognisable in the present day, both in speech and the written word, but it would take more than 150 years to achieve.

William Caxton had transferred his printing press from Bruges to Westminster, London, in 1476 and immediately caused a sensation with a reprint of a more modern version of Chaucer's *The Canterbury Tales*. Other publications followed, including some by Caxton himself, who most probably wrote in a dialect from Kent. More and more books were now being published in English, including Thomas Malory's *Le Morte d'Arthur*. Although this publication had a French title, it was written in an East Midlands English dialect of the time. It was an enormous bestseller.

Other printers started to copy Caxton and set up shop in London. One such person was Wynand 'Wynkyn' de Worde, whose publications included *The Boke of Keruynge* and *A Treatise on Fishing with a Hook*. Another printer who made his mark was Richard Pynson, who commenced printing in the early 1490s; Pynson was different from the other printers mentioned because he tended to favour printing in Chancery Standard. As such, he was appointed the king's official printer in 1509, first to Henry VII and then Henry VIII. This meant that official royal documents and decrees were being printed in a type of Standard English and were circulated through the length and breadth of the country.

The printing presses in Europe would also play their part. From 1525 William Tyndale's translation into English of the New Testament was smuggled into the country. Although banned, it was a bestseller, and the more the Catholic Church condemned it, the greater the demand and the more popular it became. There had been other translations of the Bible into English, but they had been laboriously and lovingly hand written and totalled just a few copies. Tyndale's Bible was the first ever version to be printed in English, and it was so popular that thousands were published. Other printed translations followed, most

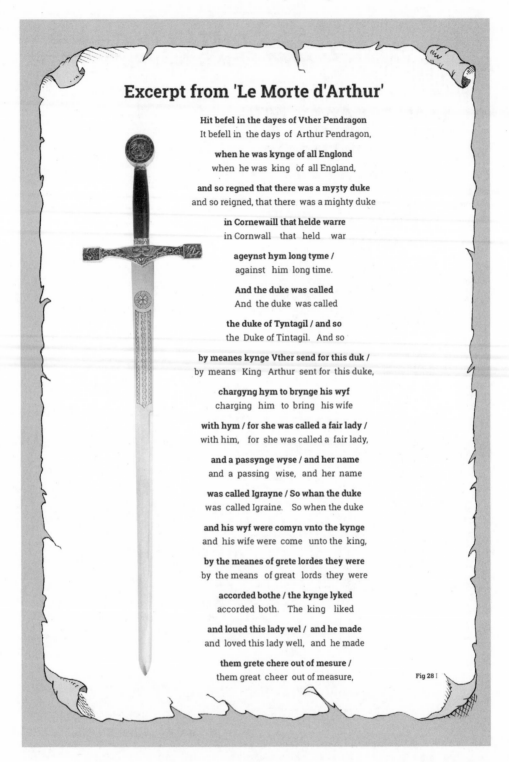

Excerpt from 'Le Morte d'Arthur'

Hit befel in the dayes of Vther Pendragon
It befell in the days of Arthur Pendragon,

when he was kynge of all Englond
when he was king of all England,

and so regned that there was a myȝty duke
and so reigned, that there was a mighty duke

in Cornewaill that helde warre
in Cornwall   that held   war

ageynst hym long tyme /
against him long time.

And the duke was called
And the duke was called

the duke of Tyntagil / and so
the Duke of Tintagil. And so

by meanes kynge Vther send for this duk /
by means King Arthur sent for this duke,

chargyng hym to brynge his wyf
charging him to bring his wife

with hym / for she was called a fair lady /
with him,   for she was called a fair lady,

and a passynge wyse / and her name
and a passing wise, and her name

was called Igrayne / So whan the duke
was called Igraine.   So when the duke

and his wyf were comyn vnto the kynge
and his wife were come unto the king,

by the meanes of grete lordes they were
by the means of great lords they were

accorded bothe / the kynge lyked
accorded both.   The king   liked

and loued this lady wel / and he made
and loved this lady well, and he made

them grete chere out of mesure /
them great cheer out of measure,

Fig 28 I

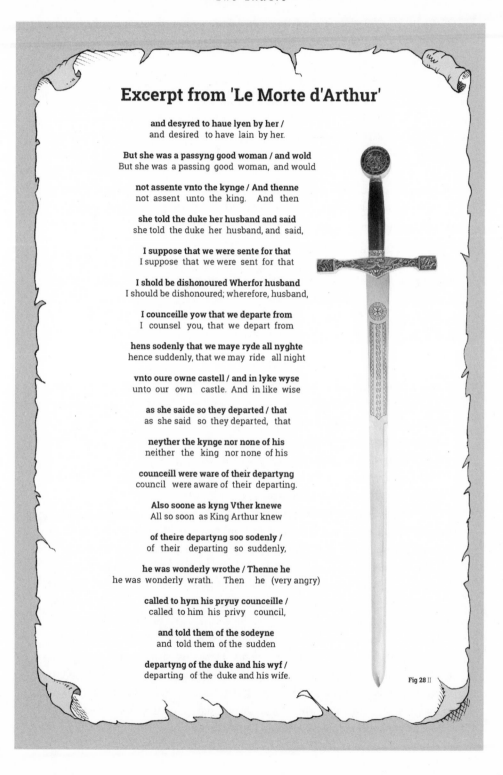

Excerpt from 'Le Morte d'Arthur'

and desyred to haue lyen by her /
and desired to have lain by her.

But she was a passyng good woman / and wold
But she was a passing good woman, and would

not assente vnto the kynge / And thenne
not assent unto the king. And then

she told the duke her husband and said
she told the duke her husband, and said,

I suppose that we were sente for that
I suppose that we were sent for that

I shold be dishonoured Wherfor husband
I should be dishonoured; wherefore, husband,

I counceille yow that we departe from
I counsel you, that we depart from

hens sodenly that we maye ryde all nyghte
hence suddenly, that we may ride all night

vnto oure owne castell / and in lyke wyse
unto our own castle. And in like wise

as she saide so they departed / that
as she said so they departed, that

neyther the kynge nor none of his
neither the king nor none of his

counceill were ware of their departyng
council were aware of their departing.

Also soone as kyng Vther knewe
All so soon as King Arthur knew

of theire departyng soo sodenly /
of their departing so suddenly,

he was wonderly wrothe / Thenne he
he was wonderly wrath.   Then he (very angry)

called to hym his pryuy counceille /
called to him his privy council,

and told them of the sodeyne
and told them of the sudden

departyng of the duke and his wyf /
departing of the duke and his wife.

Fig 28 II

notably that of King James. So important are all these versions of the Bible in helping to create a Standard English that they merit their own chapter later on.

It is generally accepted that the apostrophe began to emerge in England during the Early Modern English period. Geoffrey Troy is the French academic writer and printer who helped establish the practice of using apostrophes in a number of his French publications. It would appear that the practice was introduced into written English around 1530.

The language was written down phonetically and reflected the way people were pronouncing their words. Apostrophes were used to demonstrate when a letter or letters were being omitted during speech, for example 'I'm' instead of 'I am', and 'sha'n't' instead of 'shall not'.

The letter E was also starting to be omitted when expressing the past tense in a number of verbs and the pronunciation was shortened. Therefore, it was common in Early Modern English for the apostrophe to replace the last E in the past tense of verbs, for example *lov'd*, *kill'd* and *serv'd*. The spellings would also respond to the *-ed* being pronounced as a T, as in 'slept' instead of *sleeped* and 'crept' instead of *creeped*. A great number of verbs still have the *-ed* ending, such as 'waited', 'rested' and 'wanted'. A few archaic pronunciations have survived to the present day, for example, 'beloved' (pronounced *belove-ed*) and 'learned' (pronounced *learn-ed*).

Where verbs ended in a vowel, it became custom and practice to show the past tense with an apostrophe-D, such as *rota'd*.

Throughout history thus far, and even up to the reign of the Stuarts, the English language was written as it was said.

The possessive apostrophe took a lot longer to establish itself. In Old English, prior to the introduction of the apostrophe-S or S-apostrophe, one way of showing possession was to add an *-an* or *-n* on the end of the name. The usual way, however, was to add an *-es*. Either system of showing possession can readily be seen in English place names today. Goldsborough in North Yorkshire derives its name from *Godelesburc*, as recorded in the Domesday Book, and translates as either a stronghold or a fortified settlement (*burh*) belonging to a man called *Godel*, hence *Godeles burh,* eventually evolving into Goldsborough. Likewise, the *-es* is obvious in Luddesdown in Kent, which was first recorded in the tenth century as *Hludesduna*. This translates as a hill or down (*duna*) belonging to a man called *Hlud*. Therefore *Hludes duna* becomes Luddesdown.

However, in Haddenham in Buckinghamshire the alternative method of adding an *-n* is used. First recorded in the Domesday Book in 1086 as *Hedenham,* it derives from either a homestead settlement (*ham*) or enclosure (*hamm*) belonging to a man called *Heda,* and consequently known as *Hedan ham.*

The Vikings had also occupied great areas of land and used a similar construction to the Old English *es* for place names. Grimsby is such an example. A Viking farmstead settlement (*by*) belonging to a man called *Grimr* (*Grimes by*), it was entered in the Domesday Book as *Grimesby.* Another is Brandsby, North Yorkshire, a farmstead settlement (*by*) belonging to man called *Bradr* (*Brandes by*) abbreviated to Brandsby. In a vast number of English place names there are widespread, deep-rooted examples of Old English and Old Norse grammar showing the ownership of land, settlements, strongholds, farmsteads, homesteads and river courses.

The historic development of the possessive apostrophe replacing the *-es* with *'s* is somewhat open to conjecture. Some academics have claimed that during the Early Modern English period there was a practice of showing possession by adding the word 'has', such as 'Ruth has books'. It was thought this was rather cumbersome to say and the apostrophe replaced the *ha-* and it thus would have been abbreviated to 'Ruth's books'. There is very little evidence for this theory, however.

The more common explanation, and the most sensible, is that the possessive apostrophe quite simply replaced the *-es* in the Old English way of showing possession. Therefore, the books belonging to Ruth would have been shown as 'Ruthes books', but as the *e* was no longer pronounced, it was instead replaced with an apostrophe and once again written as it was said, 'Ruth's books'. This method of showing possession is sometimes referred to as the Saxon genitive because it is a progression from the grammatical rules of Old English. What also happened is that where a word or name ended in *-e*, such as Jane, the *-e* would remain and become Jane's books; the apostrophe did not replace the *e*.

The apostrophe-S was used for both singular and plural well into the eighteenth century. Thereafter there was a haphazard change of making apostrophe-S for the singular and S-apostrophe for the plural; it was not until the middle of the nineteenth century that English grammatical rules about the apostrophe were made more consistent.

There has been a gradual change from the Old English via Early Modern English to Modern English in its use of 'thou', 'thee', 'thy', 'thine' and 'ye'. Generally speaking, apart from some northern dialects today, spoken English has dispensed with using the majority of these words in ordinary general conversation. They have been replaced in the main with 'you', 'your' and 'yours', without any regard for customary usage within the rules of grammar. In this Early Middle English period there was a movement away from the traditional way of using these words:

'Thou' was used in the singular and would be the subject of a sentence: 'Romeo, Romeo, wherefore art thou Romeo?'

'Thee' was used in the singular and would be the object of a sentence: 'I think it's up to thee!'

'Thy' was a possessive pronoun used before a consonant: 'Hallowed be Thy name, Thy kingdom come.'

'Thine' had exactly the same meaning as 'thy' but was used before a vowel: 'Drink to me only with thine eyes.'

'Ye' used to be used more formally, and was always the plural of 'thou' when addressing a group of people: 'Come on together. Gather the harvest while ye may.'

What has gradually happened through time, from Early Modern English to the present day, is that the words 'you', 'your' and 'yours' have replaced 'thou', 'thee', 'thy', 'thine' and 'ye'. This has happened regardless of whether it's singular or plural, or whether it's formal or informal. There are, however, areas in the north of England, especially Yorkshire, where these wonderful archaic words still exist in everyday use.

It would appear that English is one of the very few European languages – if not the only one – that has the same word for singular and plural and does not alter when being used formally or informally. This is another little indication of the English language being streamlined in its modern grammar. The French, for example, have *tu* and *vous* with very strict rules on their usage. *Tu* is used in the singular informally in a friendly way to someone who is family or a close friend, whilst *vous* is used more formally. It is considered most impolite and rude if used incorrectly; however, *vous* is said in both situations if plural and when addressing a group of people. English does not have these grammatical distinctions.

During the rule of the Tudor dynasty England began to build a formidable navy, which in time would 'rule the waves' both officially and unofficially. Many explorations to the New World were sponsored

by the Tudors, particularly Henry VII and Elizabeth I. Henry VIII spent a vast fortune on building up the English navy, which arguably rose to global dominance during his reign. It would be Queen Elizabeth I who was to encourage lucrative privateering on the Spanish Main, which brought great wealth to the English queen. To be successful against the Spanish treasure fleets, the privateers needed safe havens in which to hide and operate from, and the Caribbean islands were the ideal location. The commencement of England's involvement in the barbarous slave trade began during Tudor times and, unfortunately, was another source of great wealth.

England was growing in status as a trading nation with an increase not only in its naval fleet but in its mercantile fleet as well. This growth in maritime activity meant that many other parts of the world were being discovered, new trading routes and markets were being established and overseas colonies were being founded. An unforeseen byproduct of all this naval activity were the many new words from around the globe that entered the English vocabulary during this period, which eventually became everyday parlance.

John Cabot, an Italian, was the first explorer to be sponsored by Henry VII to find a route through to China going westwards. In 1497 he landed in a 'newfound land' and gave it its name. The languages of native North Americans from the north-east of America were heard for the first time by the English party.

Henry VIII spent large amounts of his inherited wealth on building a navy that would establish England as a supreme naval powerhouse. Although the crews of these ships were mainly Englishmen, there were also many other nationalities below decks with a rich linguistic mix.

Later, in Elizabeth I's reign, John Hawkins, an adventurer and pirate, was the first Englishman to be involved in the slave trade, in 1562. Many words from West Africa, such as 'banana' and 'zebra', started to enter the English vocabulary. Trading with Spanish colonies meant that even more Spanish-based words were adapted and adopted into the English language. In 1576 Humphrey Gilbert founded Britain's 'Overseas Empire' in St John's Port, Newfoundland.

Sir Francis Drake was perhaps the most famous of Elizabeth's privateers. He rose to glory and fame for circumnavigating the world between 1577 and 1580. During this epic journey he pillaged and plundered Spanish treasure ships and South American settlements, returning to England with enormous wealth. Drake set up a temporary settlement in present-day California, called Nova Albion, which

Sir Francis Drake

ill 4

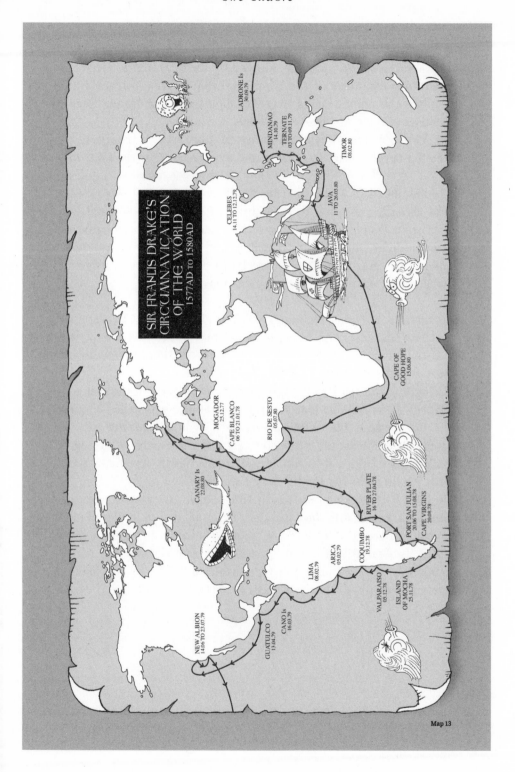

SIR FRANCIS DRAKE'S
CIRCUMNAVICATION
OF THE WORLD
1577AD to 1580AD

LADRONE Is
30.09.79

MINDANAO
14.10.79

TERNATE
03.TO 09.11.79

TIMOR
08.02.80

CELEBES
14.11 TO 12.12.79

JAVA
11 TO 26.03.80

CAPE OF
GOOD HOPE
15.06.80

MOGADOR
25.12.77

CAPE BLANCO
06 TO 21.01.78

RIO DE SESTO
05.07.80

CANARY Is
22.08.80

RIVER PLATE
16 TO 27.04.78

PORT SAN JULIAN
20.06 TO 15.08.78

CAPE VIRGINS
20.08.78

ARICA
05.02.79

COQUIMBO
19.12.78

LIMA
08.02.79

VALPARAISO
05.12.78

ISLAND
OF MOCHA
25.11.78

NEW ALBION
14.06 TO 23.07.79

CANO Is
16.03.79

GUATULCO
13.04.79

Map 13

127

included many Native Americans. More new words and phrases from the Americas would start to enter the English language, either through direct association or via those adopted by the Spanish; 'tobacco' and 'potato' are examples of the latter. In 1588 he was instrumental in defending the realm, facing overwhelming odds against the Spanish Armada and their vast fleet of galleons.

In 1584, Walter Raleigh, another of Elizabeth's favourites, was granted a royal charter to explore and annexe land for the Crown:

> Remote heathen and barbarous lands, countries, and territories, not actually possessed of any Christian Prince, or inhabited by Christian People ... and assignee for euer, with all prerogatives, commodities, jurisdictions, royalties, privileges, franchises, and preheminences, thereto or thereabouts both by sea and land, whatsoever we by our letters patents may graunt ...

The charter includes examples of how the U and V were still interchanged. It has also been suggested that the charter was written by a scribe with a London dialect, hence the spelling *preheminences,* which includes the letter H in its pronunciation.

Using this charter, Raleigh started to explore parts of the east coast of North America. The land he tried to colonise was called Virginia, after Elizabeth I, the 'Virgin Queen'. It would lead the way for subsequent colonisation during the reign of the Stuarts. Once again, through association, it would mean many North American native words would enter the English language.

In 1593 Richard Hawkins' South American voyage was immortalised in his book *Voiage into the South Sea*. This included examples of many Spanish words and phrases being adopted into the English language, as well as Arabic words the Spanish had gained from the Moors. (*Voiage of the South Sea* was republished in 1847 by the Hakuylt Society and inspired Charles Kingsley's *Westward Ho!*)

Excerpt from Charter to Sir Walter Ralegh : 1584

ELIZABETH by the Grace of God of England, Fraunce and Ireland Queene, defender of the faith, &c. To all people to whome these presents shall come, greeting.

Knowe yee that of our especial grace, certaine science, and meere motion, we haue given and graunted, and by these presents for us, our heires and successors, we giue and graunt to our trustie and welbeloued seruant Walter Ralegh, Esquire, and to his heires assignee for euer, free libertie and licence from time to time, and at all times for ever hereafter, to discover, search, finde out, and view such remote, heathen and barbarous lands, countries, and territories, not actually possessed of any Christian Prince, nor inhabited by Christian People, as to him, his heires and assignee, and to every or any of them shall seeme good, and the same to haue, horde, occupie and enjoy to him, his heires and assignee for euer, with all prerogatives, commodities, jurisdictions, royalties, privileges, franchises, and preheminences, thereto or thereabouts both by sea and land, whatsoever we by our letters patents may graunt, and as we or any of our noble progenitors haue heretofore graunted to any person or persons, bodies politique.or corporate: and the said Walter Ralegh, his heires and assignee, and all such as from time to time, by licence of us, our heires and successors, shall goe or trauaile thither to inhabite or remaine, there to build and fortifie, at the discretion of the said Walter Ralegh, his heires and assignee, the statutes or acte of Parliament made against fugitives, or against such as shall depart, romaine or continue out of our Realme of England without licence, or any other statute, acte, lawe, or any ordinance whatsoever to the contrary in anywise notwithstanding.

And we do likewise by these presents, of our especial grace, meere motion, and certain knowledge, for us, our heires and successors, giue and graunt full authoritie, libertie and power to the said Walter Ralegh, his heires and assignee, and every of them, that he and they, and euery or any of them, shall and may at all and euery time, and times hereafter, haue, take, and leade in the saide voyage, and trauaile thitherward, or to inhabit there with him, or them, and euery or any of them, such and so many of our subjects as shall willingly accompanie him or them, and euery or any of them to whom also we doe by these presents, giue full libertie and authority in that behalfe, and also to hare, take, and employ, and vse sufficient shipping and furniture for the Transportations and Nauigations in that behalfe, so that none of the same persons or any of them, be such as hereafter shall be restrained by us, our heires, or successors. . . . .

. . . . In witness whereof, we haue caused these our letters to be made patents. Witnesse our selues, at Westminster, the 25. day of March, in the sixe and twentieth yeere of our Raigne.

Fig 29

Examples of some foreign words adopted into the English Language, through trade, commerce, privateering and exploration

(from late Middle English to end of the Tudors)

Modern English word	source	English vocabulary
admiral	Arabic *amir-al* via Old French *admirail*	late 15th century
alchemy	Arabic *al-kimiyá* via Old French *admirail*	late 15th century
alcohol	Arabic *al-kuhl* via Old French	mid 16th century
algebra	Arabic *al-jabr* via Italian and Spanish	late 15th century
almanac	Arabic *al-manác* via Spanish	late 15th century
anchovy	Portuguese *anchova*	late 16th century
armada	Spanish *armata*	mid 16th century
arsenal	Arabic via Italian *arzanale*	early 16th century
bamboo	Malay *mambu* via Dutch *bamboes*	late 16th century
barricade	Spanish *barrica* via French	late 16th century
bankrupt	Italian *banca rotta*	mid 16th century
bazaar	Persian *bázár* via Ital *bazarro*	late 16th century
bravado	Spanish *bravada*	late 16th century
breeze	Portuguese *briza*	mid 16th century
ballot	Italian *ballotta*	mid 16th century
cannibal	Spanish *canibales*	mid 16th century
caravan	Persian *kárwán* via Old French *caravane*	late 15th century
carnival	Italian *carnevale*	mid 16th century
caviar	Medieval Greek *khaviar* via Italian *caviaro* via French *caviar*	mid 16th century
chess	Persian *shah* via Old French *asches*	late 15th century
comrade	Latin via Spanish *camerade*	mid 16th century
cork	Spanish/Arabic *qorq*	late 15th century

Fig 30 I

Examples of some foreign words adopted into the English Language, through trade, commerce, privateering and exploration

(from late Middle English to end of the Tudors)

Modern English word	source	English vocabulary
crew	Old French *creue*	late 15th century
design	Latin *designare* via Italian	mid 16th century
duel	Latin *duellum*	late 15th century
explore	French *explorer*	mid 16th century
hazard	Arabic *az-zahr* via Spanih *azar* via Old French *hasard*	late 15th century
horde	Turkish *ordu*	mid 16th century
infantry	French via Italian *infanteria*	late 16th century
jar	Arabic *jarra* via Old French *jarre*	late 16th century
lute	Arabic *al-'úd* via Old french *leut*	late 15th century
macaroni	Greek via Italian *maccarone*	early 16th century
machine	Greek *mēkhos* via Latin via French	mid 16th century
miniature	Italian *miniatura*	late 16th century
molasses	Portuguese *melaço*	mid 16th century
moustache	Greek *mustax* via Italian	late 16th century
passport	French *passeport*	late 15th century
progress	Latin *progressus*	late 15th century
saffron	Arabic *za'farán* via Old French *safran*	late 15th century
shock	French *choquer*	mid 16th century
syrup	Arabic *śaráb* via Old French *sirop*	late 15th century
tambourine	Persian *tambúr* via Old French *tambourin*	late 16th century
ticket	French *étiquet*	early 16th century
violin	Italian *violino*	late 16th century
vogue	Italian *voga*	late 16th century

Fig 30 II

9

The Renaissance

The Renaissance was an Italian cultural revolution that started in the mid-fourteenth century and eventually affected most of Europe. It is argued by many historians that its origins can be traced to 8 April 1341, when the Italian poet Francesco Petrarch was crowned Poet Laureate in Rome. Petrarch had rediscovered the works of Cicero, a Roman philosopher alive from 106 BC to 43 BC. The writings, sonnets and poems that Petrarch produced, which were greatly influenced by Cicero's revived philosophies, are said to have sparked off the Renaissance. The phenomenon would gather strength and not lose momentum for well over two hundred years, with a gradual petering out thereafter.

The English Renaissance lagged behind the Italian one somewhat, and took time to get going. The delayed reaction of the English ruling classes in responding to the Italian cultural and social upheaval was quite simply down to the internal conflict for control underway on the island, eventually culminating in the Wars of the Roses between the Lancastrians and the Yorkists.

The dates on which many historians agree for the English Renaissance is from the end of the Wars of the Roses in the late fifteenth century, continuing well into the seventeenth century. It would have a huge and lasting effect on spoken English. Some 10,000 to 12,000 words would be added to the English vocabulary. Though the grammatical structure of the language would hardly be affected, this represented a monumental increase in its range.

Italy had become the cultural centre of the known world for art, literature, music, architecture, scientific discoveries and humanism. The main characters in the Renaissance were most determined in rediscovering the thought of ancient Rome and Greece and resurrecting their literature, historical manuscripts and philosophies. The Renaissance artists included Donatello from Florence, Botticelli from Tuscany and, perhaps the most famous, also from Tuscany, Michelangelo. Raphael is regarded as the greatest artist during this period. The mathematicians included Ignazio Danti and Galileo Galilei.

Leonardo da Vinci (1452–1519) was perhaps the most dominant figure during this time, broadening the horizons in science, art, sculpture, engineering, biology and many other avenues of discovery. Niccolo Machiavelli was a politician, historian and writer, and his ruthless philosophy of the 'ends justifying the means' has led to the word 'Machiavellian' entering the English vocabulary. Italian Renaissance composers included Giovanni Pierluigi da Palestrina and Carlo Gesualdo. The first Renaissance architect is thought to be Filippo Brunelleschi.

The Italian Renaissance would affect practically all walks of life. Research into medicine and biology filtered through to the medical profession, which would help everyone. Although crude by today's standards, they were indeed great steps forward at the time, furthering understanding of the human body. The rich and wealthy landowners, merchants and aristocracy were sponsoring and financing this cultural change. The most influential backer was the papacy, and many popes throughout the period personally saw to it that the finances were there to maintain the momentum.

Meanwhile, back in England, the Wars of the Roses were dragging down the finances of the Crown. Taxation was high, which people could ill afford; many menfolk were engaged as soldiers in the civil war, which resulted in heavy casualties and deaths. There was indeed a great deal of unrest and poverty throughout the land. There were no finances available for such things as art, poetry, music and an English Renaissance. However, after the Battle of Bosworth Field in 1485 and the successful acquisition of the crown by Henry Tudor from Richard III, England went through a relatively calm period. The death of Richard III and the marriage of Henry Tudor to Elizabeth of York guaranteed a fairly stable and peaceful time, which in turn resulted in England becoming more prosperous and wealthy during Henry VII's reign.

It was during this period that the English Renaissance began and money was made available for the arts and sciences. Many English

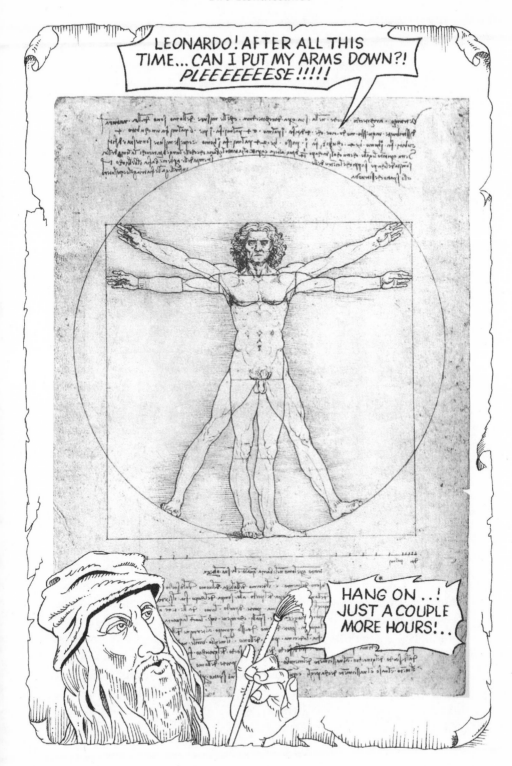

noblemen visited and stayed in Italy, only to return with new ideas and acquired fashions. Many Italian noblemen were invited to England and were entertained with a great exchange of ideas, philosophy and thinking. Artisans and merchants did exactly the same, as did writers and artists. There was a massive influx of all things Italian into the English way of life.

The momentum would increase throughout the Tudor period and carry on well into the Stuart era. Shakespeare would add to the growth of the English Renaissance by writing a number of plays wholly or partly based in Italy – *Romeo and Juliet, A Merchant of Venice, Two Gentlemen of Verona, Julius Caesar* and *Much Ado About Nothing*. The Italian influence on the English Renaissance meant that a phenomenal number of Greek and Latin words would be adopted into the English language; some 10,000 to 12,000 words entered the vocabulary.

The Renaissance was not just about poets and playwrights writing in flamboyant English. It included a scientific revolution and the subsequent discoveries that followed. It would change designs in English architecture. It would have an effect on English music, although painting and art would lag behind and be dominated by European masters. There were many contributors to the English Renaissance who helped to promote the English language and English free thinking.

The theatre was to change dramatically, quite literally, during the Elizabethan age. Previously, during the Middle English period and early time of the Tudors, the theatre had progressed from the miracle plays and mystery plays to cycles and medieval pageants. These dramatic performances were very popular and were acted in front of very large audiences, sometimes in their thousands. They were written in an English vernacular, usually pertaining to the area where they were being performed. However, due to opposition from the Church and King Henry VIII, these plays were banned, which in turn left the door wide open for the up-and-coming Renaissance dramas being performed in a more formal setting. Although the pageants made a resurgence during Mary's reign, they had had their day and never recovered; during the Elizabethan era they had practically finished, and were completely replaced with the revolutionary Renaissance plays of William Shakespeare, Ben Jonson, Christopher 'Kit' Marlowe, Thomas Kyd, Francis Bacon and others.

Some examples of Italian and Latin words entering English vocabulary during English Renaissance

Italian & Latin-based words	Modern English	Italian & Latin-based words	Modern English
absurditas	absurdity	adaptare	adapt
agilis	agile	antemna	antenna
apparare	apparatus	aquaticus	aquatic
area	area	attitudine	attitude
balcone	balcony	buffone	buffoon
capsula	capsule	carnevale	carnival
complexus	complex	conceptum	concept
concerto	concert	corridore	corridor
dislocatus	dislocate	equester	equestrian
equinus	equine	excavare	excavate
expendere	expensive	explanare	explain
factum	fact	femininus	feminine
ficticius	fictitious	focus	focus
frugalis	frugal	genius	genius
gradualis	gradual	habitualis	habitual
horridus	horrid	illicitus	illicit
infernus	inferno	insanus	insane
inventio	invention	lens	lens
manuscriptus	manuscript	marinus	marine
masculinus	masculine	meditari	meditate
militia	militia	notorius	notorious
opera	opera	orbita	orbit
paternalis	paternal	piedestallo	pedestal
pedester	pedestrian	physica	physician
premium	premium	pungent	pungent
radius	radius	solus	solo
species	species	specimen	specimen
squalere	squalor	stiletto	stiletto
taediosus	tedious	taedium	tedium
technicus	technique	temperatura	temperature
traffico	traffic	ultimatus	ultimate
ombrella	umbrella	volcano	volcano

Fig 31 I

Some examples of Greek words entering English vocabulary during English Renaissance

Greek-based words	Modern English	Greek-based words	Modern English
abax	abacus*	*akmē*	acme
akadēmeia	academy**	*agapē*	agape
agōnia	agony**	*alphabētos*	alphabet*
anatomia	anatomy*	*analusis*	analysis*
anōnumos	anonymous*	*anthologia*	anthology*
atmosphaira	atmosphere*	*atomos*	atom**
biographia	biography*	*katastrophē*	catastrophe*
khaos	chaos*	*kharaktēr*	character**
khoros	chorus*	*kōmōidos*	comedy**
klimax	climax*	*krisis*	crisis*
kritērion	criterion**	*kuklos*	cycle**
dekādos	decade	*despotēs*	despot**
diagraphein	diagram*	*diplōma*	diploma*
dogma	dogma	*dosis*	dose**
drama	drama*	*dunasteia*	dynasty**
ekkentros	eccentric*	*ekklēsiastēs*	ecclesiastic**
oikonomia	economy**	*emphainein*	emphasis*
*enthousiasmos***	enthusiasm	*epiphainein*	epiphany**
erotikos	erotic**	*aithēr*	ether**
ēthikē	ethic**	*exōtikos*	exotic
geōgraphia	geography**	*glōssa*	gloss**
grammatikē	grammar **	*gumnasion*	gymnasium*
hairesis	heresy*	*hērōs*	hero*
horizōn	horizon*	*huphen*	hyphen*
*eidōlon***	idol	*lexikon*	lexicon*
litaneia	litany**	*muthologia*	mythology**
nausia	nausea*	*paradoxon*	paradox*
paraluesthal	paralysis*	*parasitos*	parasite*
pathētikos	pathetic*	*plateia*	place**
mouseion	museum*	*orkhēstra*	orchestra*
sarkasmos	sarcasm*	*skeletos*	skeleton*
sunodos	synod*	*sustēma*	system**
theatron	theatre**	*theōria*	theory*
tragōdia	tragedy**	*trauma*	trauma

* English words with Greek origin via Latin
** English words with Greek origin via Latin then French

Fig 31 II

The main character who helped shape and characterise English Renaissance literature was Shakespeare. Not only did he epitomise this glorious age in English drama, but more importantly he also had an everlasting effect on the English language. His imaginative mind and brilliant mastery of the unfettered English language, with no prescriptive rules on grammar and a lack of consistency in spelling, meant that Shakespeare could creatively run riot with his use of words and take full advantage of the literal freedom of speech. An accumulation of all the thousands of new Renaissance Latin- and Greek-based words entering the English language via Italian had a remarkable effect on Shakespeare's creativity. It has been calculated by linguistic historians that Shakespeare introduced in excess of 1,700 of his own newly constructed words into his plays, sonnets and poems. A vast number of these words would permanently enter into the English vocabulary and appear in normal conversation.

Shakespeare was not the only writer making up words, but he fuelled the 'Inkhorn Controversy' that had erupted (an inkhorn was a container made out of a small horn that held the writer's ink and became a nickname for the new words being created).

One advocate for these so-called inkhorn words was Thomas Elyot (1490–1556), a prolific writer during the English Renaissance. Having had a classical education, he was well read in both Latin and Greek and, as such, was able to introduce many newly concocted words into the English vocabulary – some temporarily and others more lastingly. Elyot was to write a book entitled *The castel of helth gathered and made by Syr Thomas Elyot knyghte, out of the chiefe authors of physyke, wherby euery manne may knowe the state of his owne body, the preseruation of helthe, and how to instructe welle his physytion in sycknes that he be not deceyued*. This was a manual on medical matters intended for readers unfamiliar with Greek or Latin terminology. Elyot also advocated education for women so they could help stimulate their husbands' minds, be intelligent and good conversationalists, and set an example to the children. He also published one of the first English dictionaries translating Latin words into English.

George Pettie (1548–1589) was a Renaissance writer of romances. He had a classical education and supported the idea that inkhorn words should be encouraged to enrich the English vocabulary, and did so in a publication entitled *A petite pallace of Pettie, his pleasure containing many pretie histories by him set forth in comely colours and most delightfully discoursed.*

Some examples of Shakespeare's made up words

(or those he used first in printed form)

academe	accessible	accommodation	addiction
admirable	airless	amazement	arch-villain
assassination	auspicious	barefaced	baseless
bedroom	belongings	birthplace	bloodstained
bloodsucking	boldfaced	candle holder	characterless
chimney-top	circumstantial	cold-blooded	cold-hearted
countless	courtship	critical	cruel-hearted
dauntless	dawn	day's work	dewdrop
distrustful	domineering	downstairs	employer
employment	engagement	equivocal	eventful
excitement	expedience	expertness	exposure
eyeball	fairyland	fair-faced	fanged
farmhouse	far-off	fashionable	featureless
fixture	flowery	footfall	foppish
foregone	fortune-teller	foul mouthed	fretful
frugal	full-grown	generous	gentlefolk
green-eyed	gust	hobnail	hostile
hot-blooded	hunchbacked	ill-tempered	impartial
import	inaudible	inauspicious	indistinguishable
inducement	informal	invitation	jaded
lacklustre	ladybird	lament	laughable
leaky	leapfrog	loggerhead	lonely
long-legged	love letter	madcap	majestic
manager	marriage bed	misgiving	misquote

Fig 32 I

Some examples of Shakespeare's made up words
(or those he used first in printed form)

monumental	moonbeam	motionless	mountaineer
neglect	obscene	ode	outbreak
overblown	overgrowth	overview	pageantry
pale-faced	pebbled	pious	plumpy
posture	prayerbook	protester	published
puppy-dog	quarrelsome	radiance	rascally
raw-boned	reclusive	refractory	reinforcement
reliance	remorseless	restoration	restraint
retirement	revolting	roadway	rose-cheeked
rose-lipped	rumination	sanctimonious	savage
schoolboy	scuffle	self-abuse	shipwrecked
shooting star	silk stocking	silliness	skim'd milk
soft-hearted	spectacled	stealthy	stillborn
successful	suffocating	tardiness	time-honoured
title page	traditional	tranquil	transcendence
unaccommodated	unchanging	unclaimed	uncomfortable
uneducated	unfrequented	ungoverned	unhelpful
unhidden	unlicensed	unmitigated	unpolluted
unpremeditated	unpublished	unquestionable	unreal
unrivalled	unscratched	unsolicited	unsullied
untutored	unvarnished	unwillingness	upstairs
useful	useless	valueless	vulnerable
watchdog	well-behaved	well-bred	well-educated
well-read	worn out	wry-necked	zany

Fig 32 II

Shakespeare more than supported the use of inkhorns: he made it his trademark. But he was a little different to the others. A large number of his inkhorn words were derived from Latin- and Greek-based words, but many were either adopted from various English dialects or were two-word amalgamations that had not been previously used. He would also change verbs into nouns and make other grammatical changes. However, many of his inkhorn words were short-lived and did not survive.

Those academics and scholars totally against inkhorn words included Thomas Wilson, who was held in high regard not only as an academic and a scholar but also as an author, a diplomat, a judge, a privy councillor and the Dean of Durham. He is best known for two publications in particular. The first bestseller was entitled *The Rule of Reason, conteinynge the Arte of Logique set forth in Englishe* and the second and most famous of his works was *The Arte of Rhetorique*, which is believed to be the earliest comprehensive critical analysis of English rhetoric. He was against the flowery, extravagant speech and inkhorns that the English Renaissance authors and playwrights adapted from Greek and Latin. He was an advocate for a more simple way of writing and using words derived from Old English rather than from foreign countries; his work is perhaps one of the first books on plain English. *The Arte of Rhetorique* was considered a masterpiece at the time and was reprinted several times.

Another exponent of the English language and an opponent of inkhorns was Sir John Cheke (1514–1557). He was an author, statesman, privy councillor, Regius Professor of Greek at Cambridge University, and private tutor to Prince Edward, later Edward VI. Sir John made public his views on inkhorns and how the thousands of new, made-up Greek and Latin words were destroying the English language, making it pretentious and affected:

> I am of the opinion that our own tung shold be written cleane and pure, unmixt and unmangeled with borowing of other tunges; wherein if we take not heed by tijm, ever borowing and never payeing, she shall be fain to keep her house as bankrupt. For then doth our tung naturallie and praisablie utter her meaning, when she bouroweth no counterfeitness of other tunges to attire her self withall, but useth plainlie her own such shift, as nature, craft, experiens and folowing of other excellent doth lead her unto, and if she want at ani tijm (as being unperfight she must) yet let her borow with such bashfulness, that it mai appeer, that if either the

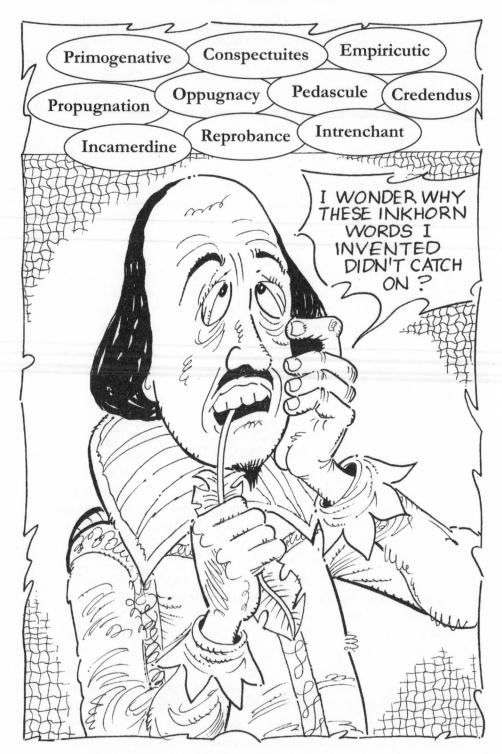

Examples of some of the inkhorn words that Shakespeare invented that did not survive

Word	Quote	Source
Affined	'.the wise and fool, the artist and unread, the hard and soft, seemed all affin'd and kin.'	Troilus & Cressida, Act 1, scene 3
Arm-gaunt	'.and soberly did mount an arm-gaunt steed.'	Antony and Cleopatra, Act 1 scene 5
Attasked	'.you are much more attask'd for want of wisdom than prais'd for harmful mildness.'	King Lear, Act 1, scene 4
Bubukles	'.his face is all bubukles, and whelks, and knobs...'	Henry V, Act 3, scene 6
Cadent	'.with cadent tears fret channels in her cheeks.'	King Lear, Act 1, scene 4
Co-mart	'.by the same co-mart, and carriage of the article design'd, his fell to Hamlet....'	Hamlet, Act 1, scene 1
Co-mate	'.now, my co-mates and brothers in exile.'	As You Like It. Act 2, scene 1
Congreeing	'.put into parts, doth keep in one consent, congreeing in a full and natural close...'	Henry V, Act 1, scene 2
Congreeted	'.that face to face and royal eye to eye. You have congreeted.'	Henry V, Act 5, scene 2
Crants	'.yet here she is allow'd her virgin crants'	Hamlet, Act 5 scene 1
Credent	'.if with too credent ear you list his songs'	Hamlet, Act 1, scene 3
Demi-natured	'.as he had been incorps'd and demi-natured with the brave beast.'	Hamlet, Act 4, scene 7
Demuring	'.with her modest eyes and still conclusion, shall acquire no honour demuring upon me.	Antony and Cleopatra, Act 4, scene 13
Directitude	'...his friends whilst he's in directitude....'	Coriolanus, Act 4 scene 5
Dispunge	'.the poisonous damp of night dispunge upon me.'	Antony and Cleopatra, Act 4 scene 9

Fig 33

mould of our own tung could serve us to fascion a woord of our own, or if the old denisoned wordes could content and ease this neede, we wold not boldly venture of unknowen wordes.

The inkhorn debate carried on as the wave of new words continued. Discrepancies and inconsistencies occurred in great numbers, when words like 'impede' would survive and the opposite *expede* would not, although 'expedient' did. Although inkhorns eventually added an even greater variation and richness to the English language, they also created more confusion.

Shakespeare liked to turn nouns into verbs and introduce even more words in that way. But he did more than just create individual words, he penned new phrases and idioms that have become part and parcel of everyday English language and conversation – still pertinent and useful 400 years later.

It is obvious with Shakespeare and other Renaissance writers that there were still no agreed standards of English grammar and spelling. Shakespeare himself would spell his own surname in at least twelve different ways. English was written phonetically and this gives a strong indication of how words were pronounced. Scholars of the time also wrote about word pronunciation. A good example is Shakespeare's spelling of the word 'film': one of the ways he spelled it was *philome*, with two distinct syllables and similar to Irish and Scottish pronunciations today; the same principle would apply to 'elm'. He uses the word *enow* for 'enough', which is a reflection of how some dialects pronounced the *ough* in 'enough' to rhyme with 'bough'. In *Othello* Act 2 Scene 3, Shakespeare spells 'alarm' as *alarum* indicating that the R is pronounced: 'Is it not an alarum to love?' A contemporary of Shakespeare, Ben Jonson, a playwright and also literary critic, writes that the R is pronounced following a vowel and refers to it as a 'doggy sound', as in *rrr*. West Country dialects today still maintain the R sound in words such as cart, farm and part as *carrt*, *farrm* and *parrt* respectively, whereas Standard English is more like an *ah* sound.

Another indication as to how people spoke at the time is the fact that Shakespeare's sonnets were of course made to rhyme, in which 'loved' rhymed with 'proved' and sounded more like *lof't* and *prof't*. Therefore the phrase 'going forth for all he's worth' would have rhymed; the word 'worth' rhymed with 'forth' with the pronunciation being similar to modern-day 'forth'. There are many more examples.

Some examples of verbs Shakespeare created, including nouns he converted

(many of these verbs are still used today)

to arouse	to barber	to bedabble	to bedazzle
to besmirch	to bet	to bethump	to blanket
to cake	to canopy	to cater	to castigate
to champion	to comply	to compromise	to cow
to cudgel	to dapple	to denote	to dishearten
to dislocate	to educate	to elbow	to enmesh
to enthrone	to glutton	to gnarl	to gossip
to grovel	to happy	to hinge	to humour
to hurry	to impede	to inhearse	to inlay
to instate	to lapse	to muddy	to negotiate
to numb	to offcap	to operate	to outdare
to outfrown	to out-Herod	to outscold	to outsell
to out-talk	to out-villain	to outweigh	to overpay
to overpower	to overrate	to palate	to pander
to perplex	to petition	to puke	to rant
to reverb	to rival	to sate	to secure
to sire	to sneak	to squabble	to subcontract
to sully	to supervise	to swagger	to torture
to unbosom	to uncurl	to undress	to unfool
to unhappy	to unmuzzle	to unsex	to widen

Fig 34

Some of Shakespeare's phrases still in common use today

All our yesterdays, Macbeth

As pure as the driven snow, Hamlet

Bated breath, The Merchant of Venice

Be all and end all, Macbeth

Brave new world, The Tempest

Dead as a doornail, Henry VI Part 2

As good luck would have it, The Merry Wives of Windsor

Break the ice, The Taming of the Shrew

In my heart of hearts, Hamlet

Cold comfort, The Taming of the Shrew and King John

Devil incarnate, Titus Andronicus

Forever and a day, As You Like It

Eaten me out of house and home, Henry IV Pt 2

Heart of gold, Henry V

Fancy-free, A Midsummer Night's Dream

Foregone conclusion, Othello

For goodness' sake, Henry VIII

Good riddance, Troilus and Cressida

Green-eyed monster, Othello

Kill with kindness, The Taming of the Shrew

Laughing stock, The Merry Wives of Windsor

In my mind's eye, Hamlet

Knock knock! Who's there? Macbeth

It's Greek to me, Julius Caesar

Live long day, Julius Caesar

More sinned against than sinning, King Lear

Love is blind, The Merchant of Venice

Milk of human kindness, Macbeth

Off with his head, Richard III

Neither a borrower or a lender be, Hamlet

Set my teeth on edge, Henry IV Pt 1

One fell swoop, Macbeth

Play fast and loose, King John

You've got to be cruel to be kind, Hamlet

Wild-goose chase, Romeo & Juliet

Seen better days, As You Like It

You can't have too much of a good thing, As You Like It

Fig 35

Excerpts from some of Shakespeare's rhyming sonnets

(The lines below would have rhymed)

v

Then were not summer's distillation left,
A liquid prisoner pent in walls of glass,
Beauty's effect with beauty were bereft,
Nor it, nor no remembrance what it was:

vi

That use is not forbidden usury,
Which happies those that pay the willing loan;
That's for thy self to breed another thee,
Or ten times happier, be it ten for one;

vii

And having climbed the steep-up heavenly hill,
Resembling strong youth in his middle age,
Yet mortal looks adore his beauty still,
Attending on his golden pilgrimage:

viii

If the true concord of well-tuned sounds,
By unions married, do offend thine ear,
They do but sweetly chide thee, who confounds
In singleness the parts that thou shouldst bear.

x

O! change thy thought, that I may change my mind:
Shall hate be fairer lodged than gentle love?
Be, as thy presence is, gracious and kind,
Or to thyself at least kind-hearted prove:

xii

When lofty trees I see barren of leaves,
Which erst from heat did canopy the herd,
And summer's green all girded up in sheaves,
Borne on the bier with white and bristly beard,

xiii

So should that beauty which you hold in lease
Find no determination; then you were
Yourself again, after yourself's decease,
When your sweet issue your sweet form should bear.

Fig 36 I

149

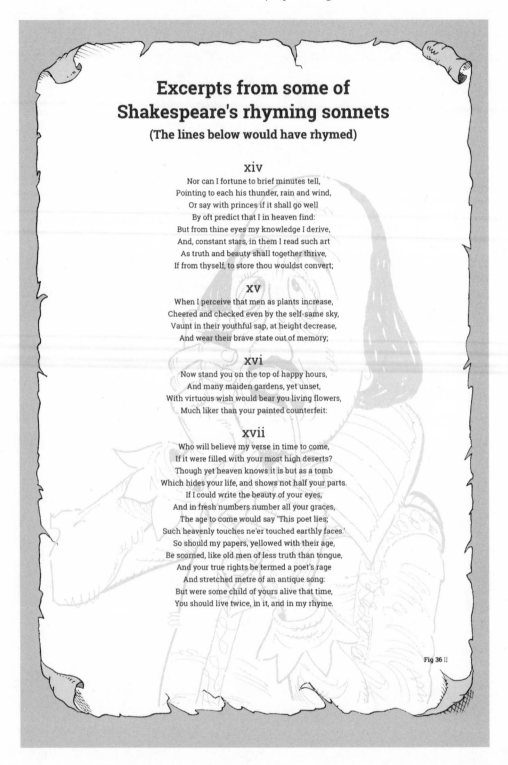

Excerpts from some of
Shakespeare's rhyming sonnets
(The lines below would have rhymed)

xiv

Nor can I fortune to brief minutes tell,
Pointing to each his thunder, rain and wind,
Or say with princes if it shall go well
By oft predict that I in heaven find:
But from thine eyes my knowledge I derive,
And, constant stars, in them I read such art
As truth and beauty shall together thrive,
If from thyself, to store thou wouldst convert;

xv

When I perceive that men as plants increase,
Cheered and checked even by the self-same sky,
Vaunt in their youthful sap, at height decrease,
And wear their brave state out of memory;

xvi

Now stand you on the top of happy hours,
And many maiden gardens, yet unset,
With virtuous wish would bear you living flowers,
Much liker than your painted counterfeit:

xvii

Who will believe my verse in time to come,
If it were filled with your most high deserts?
Though yet heaven knows it is but as a tomb
Which hides your life, and shows not half your parts.
If I could write the beauty of your eyes,
And in fresh numbers number all your graces,
The age to come would say 'This poet lies;
Such heavenly touches ne'er touched earthly faces.'
So should my papers, yellowed with their age,
Be scorned, like old men of less truth than tongue,
And your true rights be termed a poet's rage
And stretched metre of an antique song:
But were some child of yours alive that time,
You should live twice, in it, and in my rhyme.

Fig 36 II

150

Words were mainly pronounced as they were spelled and vice versa, but this principle was starting to change.

During the Middle English period through to Early Modern English the Great Vowel Shift dramatically changed the pronunciation of vowels. What also started to happen, especially during the Shakespearean period through to the mid-1600s, was a change in pronouncing certain words wherein the consonants were made silent but the spellings remained the same, and a moving away from the principle of words being spelled phonetically.

Some words ending in *-lk* such as 'talk', 'yolk' and 'folk' lost the pronunciation of the L and were pronounced as *tork, yoke* and *foke* respectively, but the spellings did not alter to match. However, 'bulk', 'sulk' and 'hulk' would continue to have the l pronounced.

Words beginning with Kn- would have been said pronouncing the K, as can be seen historically from the various spellings of the name *Knut,* which include Canute. Therefore words like 'knee', 'knife' and 'knight' went from having the K pronounced to it becoming silent, but once again the spelling did not alter to match the way the word sounded. One theory for not changing the spellings is that even more confusion could occur. The word 'know' would become 'now' and likewise 'knight' into 'night'. The dropping of the K sound before an N was peculiar to English, whereas other northern Europeans – the Dutch, Germans and Scandinavians – would carry on pronouncing the K before the N in their respective languages. Likewise the G was pronounced in words beginning with Gn- like 'gnash', 'gnaw' and 'gnarl', but during this period the G became silent in English yet remained pronounced in the German words beginning with Gn.

Many words with a T following an S, as in 'thistle', 'whistle' and 'listen', would drop the pronounced T, which would become silent instead, and the words would sound as if they had a double S in their pronunciation, in these cases *thissle, whissle* and *lissen* respectively.

The letter B on the end of some words would become silent, as in 'lamb', 'numb' and 'limb'. Before this period the B would have been pronounced. At the same time, some scholars decided to add a silent B into some words, such as 'doubt' and 'debt'; previous spellings would have been similar to *dout* and *dette*. This was done purely and simply to show the Latin origins of these words and for no other reason, in this example *dubitare* and *debitum* respectively.

The Renaissance saw a change in scientific thinking, and Sir Francis Bacon is widely recognised as the father of the scientific method in England. Bacon was a statesman and author as well as a philosopher and scientist. His scientific grounding occurred during the Elizabethan era and, along with other scholars of similar thinking, Bacon was responsible for the scientific revolution started during this time. Although new words relating to science would again start to gradually enter the English vocabulary, it was not until the time of the Stuarts that the revolution took off in a big way.

Architecture saw a change of style and fashion in the Tudor period but, once again, it was slow to take off. Hampton Court and Layer Marney Tower are examples of Renaissance architecture during the time of Henry VIII's reign with his 'palace builder in chief', Cardinal Wolsey. The Elizabethans saw a slight expansion of Renaissance building, as in Hardwick Hall, Wollaton Hall, Burghley House and a few more. New terminology relating to architecture and buildings would start to enter the English vocabulary once more, but again, it was not until the seventeenth century that Renaissance architectural design started to flourish.

The tradition of English songwriting saw practically an overnight change during the Elizabethan period, heavily influenced by the Italian movement. Previously this form of the arts had seen some change, but had remained fairly traditional. Henry VIII is attributed with 'Greensleeves', a song typical of the time. The Reformation and the Dissolution of the Monasteries had the effect of putting on hold the dramatic transformation that was to occur in English songwriting and music. During the Elizabethan era the madrigal was introduced into England and it was an instant hit. Madrigals are unaccompanied short songs with between two and eight singers, but most commonly feature between three and five. The lyrics try to express emotions in every line and the style was identifiably English but heavily influenced by the Italian tradition. It consisted of two or more parts, each having its own melody.

Nicholas Yonge was an English singer and publisher, and in 1588 published *Musica transalpina*, which was a collection of Italian madrigals that had been translated into English. It was an immediate success. It tied in at the exact moment when English poetry and plays were at a similar point of development. Renaissance English poems and sonnets easily took to the madrigal and vice versa.

This very popular form of entertainment meant that the English language was now being heard publicly in song, more so than at

Thomas Morley's most famous madrigal

Now is the Month of Maying

i
Now is the month of maying,
When merry lads are playing,
Fa la la la la la la la la,
Fa la la la la la la lah.

ii
Each with his bonny lass
Upon the greeny grass.
Fa la la la la la la la la,
Fa la la la la la la lah.

iii
The Spring, clad all in gladness,
Doth laugh at Winter's sadness,
Fa la la la la la la la la,
Fa la la la la la la lah.

iv
And to the bagpipe's sound
The nymphs tread out their ground.
Fa la la la la la la la la,
Fa la la la la la la lah.

v
Fie then! why sit we musing,
Youth's sweet delight refusing?
Fa la la la la la la la la,
Fa la la la la la la lah.

vi
Say, dainty nymphs, and speak,
Shall we play barley-break?
Fa la la la la la la la la,
Fa la la la la la la lah.

Fig 37

any other time previously. Many of the new Renaissance words and inkhorn words would also be heard for the first time in these very melodic rhyming madrigals, with audiences being able to join in with many of the choruses.

The most influential madrigal composer was Thomas Morley, who actually had the wherewithal and confidence to put Shakespeare's poetry and prose into the madrigal genre as well as into song; 'It was a lover and his lasse' is an example of the latter. In 1597 Morley published *A Plain and Easie Introduction to Practicall Musicke*, which is recognised by many critics as the most famous musical treatise ever written in the English language and a very important milestone in the history of English music. It brings together the Renaissance influence of Italian culture on Elizabethan England and takes full advantage of the versatility of the printing press. Morley wrote it in the style of a dialogue between a master and two pupils with innovative diagrams. It was an easy-to-read manual for other composers to follow and was an attempt to popularise formal music and make it more easily understood and enjoyed by people in all walks of life. He also published a collection of twenty-five different madrigals composed by twenty-three contemporary composers and named the compilation *The Triumphs of Oriana*. It was published in 1601 to celebrate the reign of Queen Elizabeth I; 'Oriana' was one of the nicknames for Elizabeth. Its derivation is complex, assocated with sunrise from the Latin for 'rising' and with gold, as in ora or ouro; hence the golden sunrise of the new Elizabethan age.

Public singing had been limited mainly to folk singing in small local gatherings. Singing in church was limited to plainsong, sung by monks or nuns in Latin, and the congregations just listened. Opera did not enter the English scene until Charles II's reign. Popular music and song being promoted during the Elizabethan era, in particular through madrigals, was therefore a revolution in itself, especially with audiences joining in the choruses. Although madrigals themselves were fashionable for a relatively short lifespan of some fifty years or so, they brought Renaissance English to the masses through the medium of unaccompanied singing. Madrigals were an important ingredient in the evolution of spoken English that is often overlooked; they helped spread the word. They have remained popular with a cappella singing groups up to the present day.

It was a Lover and his Lasse

It was a lover and his lasse,
With a haye, with a hoe and a haye nonie no,
That o'er the green corne fields did passe
In spring time, the onely prettie ring time,
When birds do sing, hay ding a ding a ding,
Sweete lovers love the spring.

Betweene the Akers of the rie,
With a haye, with a hoe and a haye nonie no,
These prettie Countrie fooles woulde lie,
In spring time, the only prettie ring time,
When birds do sing, hay ding a ding a ding,
Sweete lovers love the spring.

This Carrel they began that houre,
With a haye, with a hoe and a haye nonie no,
How that a life was but a flower,
In spring time, the only prettie ring time,
When birds do sing, hay ding a ding a ding,
Sweete lovers love the spring.

Then prettie lovers take the time,
With a haye, with a hoe and a haye nonie no,
For love is crowned with the prime,
In spring time, the only prettie ring time,
When birds do sing, hay ding a ding a ding,
Sweete lovers love the spring.

Words by William Shakespeare
Music by Thomas Morley

Fig 38

10

The Church and the Bible

The Church and the Bible had a very big influence on the English language, particualry in the time of the Tudors and Stuarts in the sixteenth and seventeenth centuries. The conflicts that raged between Protestants and Roman Catholics would see many people being tortured, hung, drawn and quartered, burnt at the stake and martyred for publishing the Bible in English and even for reading the Scriptures in English. But it would be one Bible in particular, written in English, which would become the catalyst for the beginning of a Standard English language.

As early as the tenth century, religious manuscripts were being written in English as a direct translation from the Latin. Generally speaking, however, the Roman Catholic Church would say prayers and conduct their services, such as high Mass, in Latin. The singing, if there was any, in churches, monasteries and convents would be plainsong chants in Latin up to the mid-1500s.

The Anglo-Saxons were converted to Christianity mainly during the seventh century. It was during this time that Latin would establish itself in England, both in the language of the Church and as part of Christian teaching. After visiting Rome twice to meet the Pope, King Alfred the Great was so impressed that he took things a stage further back in England by introducing Latin into the educational system of the time, which was somewhat limited and exclusive. Schooling was mainly for royalty, the Church hierarchy and the ruling classes.

Although Latin was the language of the Church, some of the religious writings and manuscripts were written in English, and there are copies

Timeline of The Bible and The Church

1380s	John Wycliffe translated Vulgate into English. Followers were known as Lollards
1401	Henry IV banned English Bibles and any English translations
1409	Archbishop Arundel of Canterbury prohibited The Bible being translated into English - any existing copies to be destroyed - Lollards still used English
1410	First of the Lollard martyrs was executed for reading scriptures in English
1428	Wycliffe's corpse exhumed and bones crushed and scattered in River Swift
1490s	Thomas Linacre compared Vulgate with original Greek manuscripts
1496	John Colet read English translation of New Testament in St Paul's Cathedral
1517	Seven parents executed in Coventry for teaching children Lord's Prayer in English
1525-6	William Tyndale's New Testament printed in English.
1532	Last of the Lollard martyrs executed
1535	Coverdale's Bible - first complete Bible in English printed in Cologne
1536	Tyndale executed as a heretic
1537	Matthew's Bible, the first to be printed in England in English under royal licence
1539	Coverdale's Great Bible placed in every church in the country by law
1549	Archbishop Cranmer's Book of Common Prayer in English was published
1553	Edward VI died and Mary I restored Catholic worship and Latin
1558	Mary died and Elizabeth I reintroduced the English Prayer Book in 1559
1560	Geneva Bible in English was printed with chapters and verses numbered
1568	Bishop's Bible, a revised version of the Great Bible published
1582	First edition of Douay-Rheims New Testament translated from Vulgate
1604	Hampton Court Conference - new English version of the Bible agreed
1610	First edition of Douay-Rheims Old Testament translated from Vulgate
1611	King James's Bible printed

Fig 39

of the Lord's Prayer in Old English. But it would take nearly 400 years before the Bible was to be handwritten in English for the first time.

In the late fourteenth century, John Wycliffe produced the first English version of the Bible, which he translated from the Latin Vulgate, the official Roman Catholic version. He was opposed to the omnipotent authority of the Pope over the Roman Catholic Church and put forward ideas for reform that included people being able to read and listen to the Bible in the vernacular. Wycliffe had quite a following: they were nicknamed Lollards, from a Dutch word meaning 'murmurers', because of the way they read their scriptures.

Wycliffe had gone against the traditional teachings of the established Catholic Church and the Lollards who supported him were persecuted. In England, King Richard II led an active campaign against heretics, which included Wycliffe's followers. Wycliffe was later punished, albeit rather belatedly, by the Pope for his translation of the Bible into English and also for his heretical preaching and teaching. John Hus, one of Wycliffe's leading followers in Europe, who actively promoted the idea that people should be able to read the Bible and Scriptures in their native language, was burned at the stake, with some of Wycliffe's Bibles being used as kindling for the fire.

Forty-four years after he had died, under orders from the Pope, Wycliffe's grave was exhumed, his bones were retrieved, and they were crushed and ground down and thrown into a nearby river. But the copies of Wycliffe's Bible that did survive were to play a significant role in promoting the English language being used in religion generally. English would be used in later translations of the Bible, religious manuscripts and teaching.

In the late fifteenth century, Thomas Linacre, an Oxford professor, personal physician to Henry VII and Henry VIII and a Greek scholar, made a very bold statement. After studying the Gospels in Greek and the Latin Vulgate he realised that there were many discrepancies and that the Latin Vulgate, which had been originally translated from the Greek, was wholly inaccurate. He pronounced when describing the Greek Gospels: 'Either this is not the Gospel or we are not Christians.' He did not actively pursue his statement as the Church continued to execute anyone reading the Bible in any language other than Latin, for example the Amersham Martyrs in 1506 and 1512. The Amersham Martyrs were active Lollards who used to meet secretly and read the Scriptures in English from a copy of Wycliffe's Bible. After being caught, to set an example to the others, their leader William Tylesworth was

Some translations
of The Lord's Prayer

Old English

Fæder ūre þū þe eart on heofonum
Sī þīn nama gehālgod
Tō becume þīn rīce
Gewurþe ðīn willa
on eorðan swā swā on heofonum
Ūrne gedæghwāmlīcan
hlāf syle ūs tōdæg
And forgyf ūs ūre gyltas
swā swā wē forgyfað ūrum gyltendum
And ne gelǣd þū ūs on costnunge
āc ālȳs ūs of yfele
Sōþlīce

John Wycliffe's version 1384AD

Oure fadir þat art in heuenes
Halwid be þi name
Ði kyngdoom cumme to
Be þi wille don
in erþe as in heuene
Yyue to vs þis dai oure breed
ouer othir substaunce
And foryyue to vs oure dettis
as we foryyuen to oure dettours
And lede vs not in to temptacioun
but delyuere vs fro yuel
Amen

William Tyndale's version 1526AD

O oure father which arte in heven,
halowed be thy name;
let thy kingdom come;
thy wyll be fulfilled
as well in erth as hit ys in heven;
geve vs this daye oure dayly breade;
and forgeve vs oure treaspases,
even as we forgeve them
which treaspas vs;
leede vs not into temptacion,
but delyvre vs ffrom yvell.
For thyne is the kingdom
and the power, and the glorye
for ever.
Amen.

King James's version 1611AD

Our father which art in heauen
Hallowed be thy name
Thy kingdome come
Thy will be done
as well in erth as hit ys in heven;
Giue vs this day our daily bread
And forgiue vs our debts
them as we forgiue
our debtors
And lead vs not into temptation
but deliuer vs from euill
For thine is the kingdome
and the power and the glory
for euer
Amen

Fig 40

burnt at the stake in 1506; his daughter was forcibly made to start the fire with a lighted torch. After much persecution from the authorities, many renounced their beliefs and returned to Catholicism. A few continued, however, and James Morden, John Scrivener, Robert Rave, Thomas Holmes, Thomas Barnard and Joan Norman were eventually burnt at the stake in 1512. Once again, one of their own children was forced to light the fire.

Those people who did renounce their Lollard beliefs were branded on their face and had to carry a symbol of a faggot at all times, knowing full well that if they ever started reading the Scriptures again in English, they would be executed in a similar way to the others. These punishments would seem more than a tad unreasonable and unfair, especially when considering the exploits some twenty years prior of an Oxford professor called John Colet. In 1496 Colet had started to read the Greek New Testament and translated it into English for his Oxford students to study and discuss, and they analysed it against the Latin Vulgate version. This proved very popular and at a later date he regularly read the New Testament in English to the congregation at St Paul's Cathedral in London. The general public was so enthusiastic to hear the New Testament in a language they could understand, that within a short space of time the news spread far and wide. There were a staggering 20,000 people in the congregation inside the cathedral with an estimation that the same number of people were outside in the street; that shows how keen people were to hear spoken English in church – in this case, the demand so great they filled a cathedral. How did Colet get away with it? His father was the Mayor of London and as a result Colet had connections in some very high places, including those in royal circles as well as the king himself; without these links, he would have gone the same way as the Amersham Martyrs and would have been publicly burnt alive.

It would be a quarter of a century before another gigantic breakthrough for the English language. In 1525 William Tyndale published, for the very first time, the New Testament in English. As this was against Catholic teaching, and England was still a Catholic stronghold, he printed it in a more Protestant-friendly northern Europe. It was an immediate bestseller and copies were smuggled into England by the thousands. The vast majority were burned but many copies survived and became the basis for other English versions to follow. He was undoubtedly a master scholar and spoke several languages fluently; many academics believe Tyndale to be the 'architect

Examples of some everyday phrases originating from The Bible

A broken heart	*Psalm 34 v18*	The Lord is nigh unto them that are of a broken heart.
A cross to bear	*Luke 14 v27*	And whosoever doth not bear his cross, and come after me cannot be my disciple.
Labour of love	*Hebrews 6 v10*	For God is not unrighteous to forget your work and labour of love, which ye have shewed toward his name ...
Thorn in the flesh	*2 Corinthians 12 v7*	...there was given to me a thorn in the flesh..
Two-edged sword	*Proverbs 5 v4*	But her end is bitter as wormwood, sharp as a two-edged sword.
Can a leopard change his spots?	*Jeremiah 13 v23*	Can the Ethiopian change his skin, or the leopard his spots?
Eye to eye	*Isaiah 52 v8*	...with the voice together shall they sing: for they shall see eye to eye, when the Lord shall bring again Zion
Fall from grace	*Galatians 5 v4*	Christ is become of no effect unto you, whosoever of you are justified by the law; ye are fallen from grace.
He who lives by the sword, dies by the sword	*Matthew 26 v52*	Then said Jesus unto him, 'Put up again thy sword into his place, for all they that take the sword shall perish by the sword.'
Put your house in order	*2 Kings 20 v1*	Thus saith the Lord, 'Set thine house in order, for thou shalt die and not live.'
Sour grapes	*Jeremiah 31 v30*	But every one shall die for his own iniquity: every man that eateth the sour grape, his teeth shall be set on edge.
The fat of the land	*Genesis 45 v18*	...I will give you the good of the land of Egypt, and ye shall eat the fat of the land.
The spirit is willing, the flesh is weak	*Matthew 26 v41*	Watch and pray, that ye enter not into temptation: the spirit is willing but the flesh is weak.
Put words in someone's mouth	*2 Samuel 14 v3*	And come to the king and speak on this matter to him. So Joab put the words in her mouth.
Wits' end	*Psalm 107 v27*	They reel to and fro, and stagger like a drunken man, and are at their wits' end.

Fig 41

Examples of some everyday phrases originating from The Bible

The last shall be first	*Matthew 20 v16*	So the last shall be first, and the first last: for many are called, but few are chosen.
Sign of the times	*Matthew 16 v3*	O ye hypocrites, ye can discern the face of the sky; but can ye not discern the signs of the times?
The powers that be	*Romans 13 v1*	...the powers that be are ordained of God.
Eat, drink and be merry	*Luke 12 v19*	And I will say to my soul, you have plenty of goods stored up for many years.....Eat, drink and be merry!
A man after my own heart	*Acts 13 v22*	...I have found David the son of Jesse, a man after mine own heart.
Left hand know what the right hand does	*Matthew 6 v3*	But when thou doest alms, let not thy left hand know what thy right hand doeth.
The salt of the Earth	*Matthew 5 v13*	You are the salt of the Earth.
Filthy lucre	*Titus 1 v11*	Whose mouths must be stopped, who subvert whole houses, teaching they ought not, for filthy lucre's sake
	1 Timothy 3 v3	Not given to wine, no striker, not greedy of filthy lucre; but patient, not a brawler, not covetous.
Fall flat on your face	*1 Corinthians 10 v12*	Don't be so naïve and self-confident. You are not exempt. You could fall flat on your face as easily as anyone else.
Land of the living	*Psalm 27 v13*	I had fainted, unless I had believed to see the goodness of the Lord in the land of the living.
Fleshpots	*Exodus 16 v3*	...when we sat by the flesh pots, and when we did eat bread to the full ...
Go the extra mile	*Matthew 5 v41*	And whoever compels you to go one mile go with him two.
Fight the good fight	*1 Timothy 6 v12*	Fight the good fight of faith
The patience of Job	*James 5 v11*	You have heard of the patience of Job and you have seen the Lord's purpose.
Let there be light	*Genesis 1 v3*	And God said, 'Let there be light'
Let my people go	*Exodus 5 v1*	Thus saith the Lord God of Israel, 'Let my people go'.

Fig 41 II

of the English language'. His English Bible introduced new words and phrases into the English language and was the foundation for the King James Bible.

Tyndale remained in Europe for safety, but continued to be a prolific writer. In 1528 he published *The Obedience of a Christen man and how Christen rulers ought to govern wherein also if thou mark diligently thou shalt find eyes to perceive the crafty convience of all iugglers*. It advocates that a king should be the head of the Church and not the Pope, which promoted the idea of the Divine Right of Kings. It is thought by many that this publication later heavily influenced Henry VIII's decision to denounce papal rule for himself to become Supreme Head of the Church in England, for which Parliament passed the Act of Supremacy in 1534. It is also believed that Henry had a copy of Tyndale's translation of the Bible, which he studied at great length. However, prior to the Act of Supremacy, Tyndale had made the mistake of going against the king by publishing *The Practyse of Prelates*, which totally opposed Henry's marriage to Catherine of Aragon being annulled. Henry's anger was obvious: he asked Charles V, the Holy Roman Emperor, to apprehend Tyndale and escort him to England to be tried for heresy or treason. Charles V did not respond favourably, so Henry instructed spies to flush out Tyndale, who was eventually apprehended in Antwerp in 1535 by imperial authorities of the Holy Roman Empire. He was tried for heresy, found guilty and condemned to death; he was tied to the stake, garrotted and burned. His dying words are reputed to have been, 'Oh Lord! Open the King of England's eyes!'

Despite his cruel execution, Tyndale still had a great influence on the style of English that would be used in future editions of the Bible. Many of the translations he made have entered the English language and become everyday phrases, including a line in a popular protest song penned by Bob Dylan, 'The Times They Are A-Changin'. Tyndale's translation of Matthew 20:16 includes 'So the last shall be first and the first last ...', which Dylan adapted to 'and the first one now will later be last ...'

The sad irony is that whilst Henry VIII repudiated Tyndale, he authorised Myles Coverdale to publish the Great Bible in English. Coverdale based it on Tyndale's version and it was distributed throughout the land.

Many academics agree that William Tyndale was a rare genius with the ability to write in such a fashion that everyone could

THE GREAT BIBLE

ill 5

understand what he had written, whether they were reading his manuscripts or listening to them being read. He is acknowledged to have had an effortless and uncluttered style with an easy turn of phrase, which only comes with a complete command of the language and a sensitive and comprehensive understanding of the listener. His translations helped pave the way for a subsequent explosion of religious writings, translations and manuscripts that were printed and published in English, including several versions of the Bible. He is put alongside Chaucer and Shakespeare in importance when discussing and analysing the history of the English language. Tyndale would greatly influence, although posthumously, the creation of a uniformity in the language that would eventually lead to Standard English some two centuries later.

In 1539, four years after Tyndale's execution, Myles Coverdale, as authorised by Henry VIII, produced the Great Bible, so called because of its enormous size, being over fourteen inches in height. There were seven editions printed between April 1539 and December 1541. The second edition, in 1540, and those thereafter were also known as 'Cranmer's Bible' because the preface was written by him as Archbishop of Canterbury, with the advice that it should either be listened to or read by everyone throughout the kingdom. The following is excerpted from Thomas Cranmer's very long preface:

Who is it, that redying or hearing read in the gospel ... can perceive nothing except he have a master to teache hym what it meaneth. Likewyse, the sygnes and myracles with all other histories the doyings of Christe or his apostles, who is there, of so symple wyt and capacitie, but he may be able to preceyve and understand them? ... Take the bookes into thyne hands, reade the whole story, and that thou understandest, kepe it well in memory: that then understandest not, reade it agayne, and agayne: yf thou can neyther so come by it, counsarle with some other that is better learned. Goe to thy curate and preacher, shewe thy selfe to be desyrous to knowe and learne. And I doute not but God seeying thy dilygence and readyness (yf no manne els teache thee) wyll hymselfe vouchsafe with holy spryte to illumynate thee, and to open unto thee that whiche was locked from thee ...

Although the Great Bible was written by Myles Coverdale, his work was executed under the scrutiny of Lord Thomas Cromwell, Vicar General and Vicegerent but also Principal Secretary to King Henry VIII, along with many other titles. Coverdale's version relied heavily on Tyndale's translation, with certain sections being deleted – passages that had been objected to by a number of the bishops. Coverdale also completed the unfinished work of Tyndale by finishing the translation of the Old Testament, but this time from the Vulgate and German translations and not from the Greek.

Cromwell instructed all clergy that a copy of the Great Bible should be made available in all churches and cathedrals for the general public to study and read. An excerpt from the modernised version of his instructions reads as follows:

> Item, That ye shall provide ... one book of the whole Bible of the largest volume in English, and the same set up in some convenient place within the said church, that ye have cure of, whereat your parishioners may most commodiously resort to the same, and read it the charges of which book shall be rateably borne between you, the parson and parishioners aforesaid, that is to say, the one half by you, and the other half by them.
>
> Item, That ye shall discourage no man privily or apertly [openly] from the reading or hearing of the said Bible, but shall expressly provoke, stir, and exhort every person to read the same, as that which is the very lively word of God, that every Christian person is bound to embrace, believe and follow, if he look to be saved; admonishing them, nevertheless, to avoid all contention and altercation therein, and to use an honest sobriety in the inquisition of the true sense of the same, and to refer the explication of the obscure places to men of higher judgement in Scripture.

Subsequently, every church and cathedral in the land had an English Bible. It was usually chained to a wall or a strong oak beam to avoid theft. This provision of the scriptures for all was a watershed in the history of the English language; English was now becoming the official language of the Church and very quickly replacing Latin.

Henry VIII was a devout Catholic and his reasoning for changing his mind on wanting the Bible in English was purely for political rather than religious reasons. Henry's divorce from Catherine had not been agreed by the Pope. As previously mentioned, it is thought by many that Henry used the principles of the Divine Right of Kings, as argued by William Tyndale in *The Obedience of a Christen man,* to uphold his actions following the Pope's lack of support, a supremely ironic turn of events. He could also justify being head of the Church in England using Tyndale's political and religious ideology. Henry could add weight to his argument because he had previously earned the title of 'Defender of the Faith' from the Pope himself for his public opposition to Protestantism. In effect, by declaring himself as the head of the Church, Henry created a new branch of Christianity that was neither Catholic nor Protestant, or at least not Protestant in the way the term was understood on the continent; it would become known as the Anglican Church, or the Church of England. So his authorisation of the Great Bible to be written in English and to be read and listened to across the nation was one of the first things he did to show his authority and snub the Pope. English would become the voice of the Church. It would appear that Tyndale's dying words had been heard.

The effect the Great Bible had on the population as a whole was not only to fuel the ideology of the English Reformation. Its word was received by a higher percentage of the population than for any other printed material previously. The people in many parts of England, especially the regions away from London, Cambridge and Oxford, were hearing a style of English that had never been heard before. The Great Bible was largely based on Tyndale's eloquence and use of the English language in his original translation. It also meant that an English standard was starting to evolve, which was maintained in the many other versions of the Bible that followed, based on Tyndale's original translation.

Many English-language historians have rated Tyndale so highly that they have stated that if there had not been a Tyndale there would not have been a Shakespeare. Over 1,200 allusions to the Bible by Shakespeare – if not more – originated from translations influenced by Tyndale, especially in the later Geneva Bible. Others believe that Shakespeare was such a genius that he would have still made a massive impact on the English language in any case.

During Henry's kingship the Reformation would gather strength, so much so that England drew even further away from Catholicism. The Dissolution of the Monasteries between 1536 and 1541 was the most obvious manifestation of this breakaway. Monasteries, priories, convents and friaries had their income appropriated and assets disposed of, and many buildings and their contents were vandalised and destroyed. Most of the money raised was to fund Henry's war

against France. Arguably, Henry was hiding behind the shield of religion to promote his own secular and political gains.

Two years after Henry VIII's death, during the reign of Edward VI, perhaps one of the most important printed documents in the history of the English language would be published. In 1549 the *Act of Uniformity of Service and Administration of the Sacraments throughout the Realm* established for the first time a *Book of Common Prayer* to be printed in English. Archbishop Thomas Cranmer was instrumental in its publication. The text was essentially a translation and bringing together of the various versions of the Missal into one official standardised English version; they had all previously been written in Latin and contained instructions and texts for the various religious celebrations, like Mass, and other acts of worship. The Act was quite particular and stated that all places of worship had to use the *Book of Common Prayer* and no other:

> And that all and singular ministers in any cathedral or parish church or other within the realm of England ... shall ... be bound to say and use Matins, Evensong, celebration of the Lord's Supper, commonly called the Mass, and administration of each of the sacraments, and all their common and open prayer, in such order and form as is mentioned in the said book, and none other or otherwise.

The Act was also very specific as to penalties for those members of the clergy not using the new English prayer book. Upon first offence the sentence by today's standards would be very harsh indeed: total loss of earnings for one year, which was forfeited to the Crown, plus six months in gaol without bail. Conviction on the second offence was even stiffer: total loss of livelihood plus another year in gaol. A third offence meant life imprisonment.

English was now being used wholeheartedly within the Church; there were some objections from some devout, unerring Catholics, but in the main, English had taken hold. There was one significant delay to come, however, when Mary became queen. She was an extremely strict and devout Roman Catholic, and during her reign some of the previous acts were repealed in an attempt to return England to Catholicism, with Latin being used again in church. Many Protestants feared for their lives and fled to Geneva, as Switzerland was the only safe haven for them. Many who were not able to escape were burnt at the stake in great numbers, some were were hanged and quartered, too. Using the English language in church and prayer had become a perilous occupation. (Though to be fair to 'Bloody Mary', her father had far more of his subjects put to death than she did.)

Those that escaped to Geneva included Myles Coverdale, who, together with a few contemporaries – William Wittingham, Christopher Goodman, Anthony Gilbey, Thomas Sampson and William Cole – produced a Bible for the English Protestants to read whilst based in Switzerland. This Bible became known as the Geneva Bible and once again was based very largely on Tyndale's translations, but it was also unique for a number of reasons. Firstly, all the verses were numbered as well as all the chapters for easy reference, and secondly, all the books in the Bible had comprehensive study notes and references appended in the margins. It also included maps and many illustrations. One very big selling point for this particular Bible is that it was printed in the easier to read Roman typeface as opposed to an older, more elaborate type. Not only that, it was printed in various sizes, including less expensive and smaller editions, and ones more manageable for everyday use, including a pocket-size version.

When Mary died, her sister Elizabeth came to the throne and the course of history would change yet again. The Geneva Bible began to be printed in England and would go on to nearly 150 editions. To begin with, it became the most popular version of the Bible, even more so than James I's version that was to follow. It was the Geneva Bible that was taken by the Pilgrim Fathers and Puritans to the New World. It is known that Shakespeare certainly had a copy of the Geneva Bible and from it drew many direct and indirect allusions and metaphors.

It is easy to compare Tyndale's use of the English language in all the Bibles based on his original translations and the English used by Shakespeare in his plays, poetry and sonnets. Both introduced new words into everyday English vocabulary that are still in use today. But Tyndale's English was more grammatically structured, having been translated from the more strictly structured languages of ancient Greek and Latin. Through these sources, he inadvertently created a more consistent standardised form of English. Tyndale also used simple language, knowing that the Bible would be read out loud with many people listening. Shakespeare, however, used the lack of official uniformity in the language and ran riot, taking full advantage of an ambiguous, untamed language. He penned wonderfully elaborate storylines, with plots and sub-plots, and included a generous use

Myles Coverdale

ill 6

of those imaginative, ingenious inkhorn words. Both writers can be described as brilliant and unique – they are two of the small group of people through history who can be said to have been hugely instrumental in transforming the English tongue into the beautiful, rich language it is today.

It has been suggested that during the Elizabethan era one of the biggest steps in the evolution of a Standard English language resulted from the *Acte for the Uniformitie of Common Prayoure and Dyvyyne Service in the Churche, and the Adminstration of the Sacramentes,* passed in 1559. This Act officially reinstated the *Book of Common Prayer* and was Archbishop Cranmer's revised version. It was to be the one and only prayer book for use in all churches. This new ruling went a stage further and stated that everyone should attend church at least once a week or else be heavily fined. This part of the law was to be in force for a good number of years and meant that everyone throughout the nation would be listening to the style of English used in the Bible and the *Book of Common Prayer.* People would hear this style of English on a weekly basis for many years, and it would thus become familiar to them. Other revised versions of the prayer book followed, including a version re-issued in 1762 by John Baskerville. In this way a standard in English grammar was beginning to slowly emerge; it would take another two centuries before it fully evolved and eventually became established as Standard English. A standard pronunciation evolved at the same time.

During Elizabeth's reign a revised Great Bible was published, and although there were nearly twenty publication runs between 1568 and 1606, this version of the Bible, commonly referred to as the 'Bishops' Bible', was not very popular and was largely disregarded. The Geneva Bible proved to be too popular to replace.

The next great step in laying a foundation for Standard English was King James I's Bible, first published in 1611. The king and Archbishop Bancroft, at a meeting in 1604, decided how the Bible was to be translated. Rather than being based on just one scholar's translation, it would be compiled by a number of eminent scholars, conversant with the ancient languages, and which would result in a universally agreed and accurate translation of the Bible in English. Fifty translators were definitely selected, although there may have been as many as fifty-four or even more. They were split into six companies: the First and Second Westminster Companies, the First and Second Oxford Companies and the First and Second Cambridge Companies. Each company would

THE BOOK OF COMMON PRAYER

The BOOK of
Common Prayer,
And Administration of the
SACRAMENTS,
AND OTHER
RITES and CEREMONIES
OF THE
C H U R C H,
According to the Use of
The CHURCH of ENGLAND:
TOGETHER WITH THE
P S A L T E R
OR
PSALMS of DAVID,
Pointed as they are to sing or said in Churches.

CAMBRIDGE,
Printed by JOHN BASKERVILLE, Printer to the University;
by whom they are told and by B. DOD Bookseller,
in Ave Mary Lane, London, MDCCLXII.

ill 7

look at a different number of books, for example the First Westminster Company translated the first twelve books of the Old Testament whilst the Second Oxford Company translated the Gospels, the Acts of the Apostles and Revelation.

During the first year, from 1605 to 1606, the translators were purely involved in private research. For the next three years their findings were put together, argued over, discussed and finally agreed upon. In 1610 it went to the printers and was issued in the following year. It was sixteen inches tall and was to be nailed to every pulpit in the land; a year later a pocket-sized version was also produced.

Fifty or so eminent scholars had translated from ancient scriptures and compared their translations with those made previously, with a most remarkable outcome. Roughly 90 per cent of the New Testament in the King James Bible corroborated Tyndale's translation without giving him due credit. Similarly, over 80 per cent of Tyndale's unfinished translation of the Old Testament was also substantiated in the King James version. Therefore, 80 to 90 per cent of the King James Bible is in agreement with Tyndale's previous translations – an indication that one man alone was equal to fifty eminent scholars, which truly endorses Tyndale's genius and the role he has played in the evolution of Standard English.

The punctuation marks used in these early editions of James's Bible were based on the work of John Hart, a mid-sixteenth-century English grammarian. Hart had tried unsuccessfully to reform the chaotic and illogical English language with such books as *The Opening of the Unreasonable Writing of Our Inglish Toung*. He also tried, again unsuccessfully, to introduce an alphabet that had extra letters showing more phonetic characters. He did achieve the distinction, however, of introducing a punctuation system that he had adopted from Renaissance Europe, which is the basis of the punctuation used today. He introduced seven basic marks: the comma, the exclamation mark, the colon, the full stop, the question mark, and round and square parentheses.

Although the King James Bible had several editions, it would take a good number of years before it overtook the Geneva Bible in popularity. The King James version has often been referred to as the most accurate translation of the Bible and has been published in various editions for over 400 years. *The Book of Common Prayer* has also stood the test of time and is still the basis for ceremonies and celebrations in the Church of England today. The structure of the

Bible Comparisons of John, Chapter 3 Verse 16

Anglo-Saxon 995AD
God lufode middaneard
swā Þæt hē sealde hys āncennedan Sunu
Þæt nān ne forwurðe Þe on hyne gelýfð
ac hæbbe Þæt ēce līf

Wycliffe 1380AD
For God louede so the world
that he ȝaf his oon bigetun sone
that ech man that biliueth in him perische not
but haue euerlastynge lijf

Tyndale 1534AD
For God so loveth the worlde
yt he hath geven his only sonne
that none that beleve in him shuld perisshe
but shuld have everlastinge lyfe

Great Bible 1539AD
ffor God ſo loued ye worlde
that he gaue his only begottē ſonne
that whoſoeuer beleueth in him chulde not periſh
but haue euerlaſtyng lyfe

Geneva Bible 1560AD
For God ſo loued the worlde
that he hathe giuen his onely begotten Sōne
that whoſoeuer beleueth in him ſ hulde not periſh
but haue euerlaſting life

Rheims Bible 1582AD
For ſo God loued the vvorld
that he gaue his only-begotten ſonne:
that euery one that beleeueth in him periſh not
but may haue life euerlaſting

King James 1611AD
For God so loued Þe world
that he gaue his only begotten Sonne
that whosoeuer beleeueth in him should not perish
but haue euerlasting life.

Fig 42

English language within the Bible and *The Book of Common Prayer* eventually had a big influence in the shaping of a Standard English from its Chancery Standard roots. The formation of the Companies from Westminster, Oxford and Cambridge, although disbanded after their great translational work, was prototypical of a Standard English triangle that had unofficially been created. Most of the scholars and academics who helped fashion a nationally accepted grammar came from London and the universities of Oxford and Cambridge. In addition to this, most of the printing presses were based in London, and as a result the London accent became the most dominant force in this triangle.

Although the Bible and *The Book of Common Prayer* played a huge part in shaping a standard English language, it was about to take on other dimensions during the Stuart dynasty.

11

The Stuarts and the Commonwealth

James I succeeded Elizabeth and the Stuart dynasty began, lasting for over one hundred years apart from the Interregnum between the two king Charles. By the end of the Stuart era the English language would have continued in its evolution, sometimes in a way it had never done before, and the change would again be the subject for discussion by learned academics and scholars.

The King James Bible was a massive step in consolidating an English style and construction, whilst Shakespeare and some of his contemporaries continued to write in a free and unshackled manner. To harness these two extremes would take over 200 years, and even then there would be disagreements.

Whilst a standard in English was starting to emerge, the differing regional dialects had become firmly established and deep rooted. James I himself had a Scottish accent, which was secretly ridiculed at court.

The English language thus far had resulted from an eclectic mix of tongues: Celtic Britons and various European invaders, mainly with Germanic and Scandinavian roots, and some Norman-French and Breton to add to the melting pot. There was no uniformity as to where these people would settle, and each region of England would have a different mixture of these various settlers and this would occur at the county level as well.

An example of this mix can be shown by a people 'cake recipe' for Suffolk. It shows proportionally the makeup of each invading force that settled in Suffolk together with with those Britons who did not flee westwards and stayed behind (right). Each county would have very similar ingredients, if not the same, but the amounts would differ every time. Essex's cake compared with Suffolk's would see a reversal of the Angle and Saxon measures. Yorkshire and the North East would be heavier on the Dane and the Angle and less on the Saxon, with slight adjustments to the other ingredients. The West Country would have more Saxon and Celtic Briton, and the Midlands would see a more uniform mix of Angles, Saxons and Danes.

If the weights of the ingredients are altered when baking a cake, then the cake will end up different each time. Likewise, each county with its varying amounts will end up with a different result. These differences will include some unique regional vocabulary and grammar, spoken with a particular accent; these three elements make up a dialect.

Dialects are not a lazy way of speaking English. Their roots go back much further than Standard English and they are full of ancient words and phrases, many of which are from our Germanic-Viking beginnings. The study of dialects is essential in tracing back our English-speaking roots; they are steeped in ancient history and form part of our linguistic heritage.

With the lack of a national standard there were still many variances in spelling and grammar, even though there were numerous well written and well structured editions of the Bible. Even James I's version had variations in spelling and some differences in phraseology compared with the popular Geneva Bible. The English language was unfettered and untamed.

The effects of the English Renaissance on English literature continued during the Stuart period with the inkhorn debates still raging on. In 1604, an attempt was made by a schoolmaster called Robert Cawdrey to try and explain what some of these new words meant in simple English. He is credited with publishing the first alphabetical English dictionary. He was very much on the anti-inkhorn side of the debate and is quoted as saying that those adopting foreign words 'forget altogether their mother's language so that if some of their mothers were alive, they were not able to tell or understand what they say'. He also said that 'far journied gentlemen pouder their talke with oversea language'. The dictionary's full title is *A table alphabeticall conteyning and teaching the true writing, and vnderstanding of hard usuall English words, borrowed from the Hebrew, Greeke, Latine, or French, &c. With the interpretation thereof by plaine English words, gathered for the benefit & helpe of ladies, gentlewomen, or any other vnskilfull persons.*

SUFFOLK CAKE MIX

5lb / 2.5kg .... Angles

1½ lb / 700gms ... Danes

1½lb / 700gms ....Celtic Britons

½ lb / 200gms .... Saxons

½ lb / 200gms .... Normans

1 x tablespn ...... Frisians

2 x teaspns .... Flemings

1 x teaspn ....Jute

1 x teaspn ....Bretons

1 x pinch .... Dutch

Fig 43

Whereby they may the more easilie and better vnderstand many hard English wordes, vvich they shall heare or read in scriptures, sermons, or elswhere, and so be made to vse the same aptly themselues. The first edition of this dictionary contained just over 2,500 words and proved very popular, so much so that three more editions would subsequently be printed, each time containing more words than the previous edition, culminating in slightly more than 3,250 in the fourth edition in 1617.

Despite their popularity, Cawdrey's dictionaries had little effect on the language but, by a strange quirk of fate, they coincided with the English alphabet finally being established as we know it today, with its twenty-six letters. The U and V were finally separated and the U became the vowel and the V the consonant. Previously there was the convention of using the V only as the initial letter of a word, for example *vsual* for 'usual' and *haue* for 'have'; likewise, the I became the vowel and J the consonant. It is interesting to note that the modern Italian alphabet consists of twenty-one letters, with the J, K, W, X and Y only being used in loan words like 'judo' and 'karate'. The Danish and Norwegian alphabets, however, have twenty-nine letters.

Other dictionaries followed *A Table Alphabeticall* ..., but it was not until 1656, during the time of the Commonwealth, that a serious contender for a proper dictionary was published. Thomas Blount produced his *Glossographia* with more than 11,000 words. It went further than Cawdrey's dictionary and included words from science, medicine, mathematics and other specialised subjects, along with words imported by overseas merchants and traders. It went another significant step; Blount is credited with compiling the first English etymological dictionary showing the origins of words.

In 1656 Edward Philips published *The New World of English Words*, which was, in the main, a direct copy of Blount's dictionary from two years earlier. A dispute ensued between the two, but it generated great interest in lexicography and more dictionaries followed. Instead of clarifying and standardising the English language, it had the reverse effect. Some 100 years after Blount's *Glossographia* was printed, Lord Stanhope, English statesman and man of letters, in a letter to his son in 1754, bemoaned the state of the lexicographical nation:

> I cannot help thinking it is a sort of disgrace to our nation, that hitherto we have no standard of our language; our dictionaries at present being more properly what our neighbours the Dutch and the Germans call theirs, – word-books, – than dictionaries, in the superior sense of that title ...

CAWDREY'S DICTIONARY

A

Table Alphabeticall, con-
tayning and teaching the true
writing and vnderſtanding of hard
uſuall Engliſh words, borrowed from
the Hebrew, Greeke, Latine,
or French, &c.

With the Interpretation therof by
plaine Engliſh words, gathered for the
benifit and help of all unſkilfull perſons.

Whereby they may themore eaſily and
better underſtand many hard Engliſh words,
which they ſhall heare or read in Scriptures,
Sermons, or elſe where and alſo be made
able to uſe the ſame aptly themſelves.

Setforth by R.C. and newly corrected,
and much inlarged with many words
now uſe.

The 3. Edition.
Legere, & nin intelligere, neglegereeſt.
As good not to read, as not to underſtand.

LONDON
Printed by T.S. for Edmund Weaver, and are
to be ſold at his ſhop at the great North
dore of Paules Church. 1613.

ill 8

He also went on to write, 'It must be owned that our language is at present in a state of anarchy.'

It was Ben Jonson, playwright, literary critic, poet and grammarian, who compiled the first serious attempt to explain English grammar, in his book entitled *The English Grammar made by Ben Ionson* [sic], which had the subtitle *For the benefit of all Strangers, out of his observation of the English Language now spoken, and in use.* It was published in 1640, three years after Jonson had died. The book is unique and gives descriptions of each vowel and consonant, and includes the pronunciation of vowels, consonants and diphthongs, as well as instructions on grammar. An example of his painstaking approach is the way he explains how the letter 'I' was pronounced: 'I is of a narrower sound than the e, and uttered with less opening of the mouth, the tongue brought back to the palate, and striking the teeth next to the cheek teeth.' When describing how the letter C should be pronounced, Jonson makes reference back to the English Saxons. It is obvious from the text that he is not too enamoured of this letter:

C. Is a letter, which our forefathers might very well have spared in our tongue; but since it hath obtained place both in our writing and language, we are not now to quarrel with *orthography* or *custom*, but to note the powers.

Before a, u, and o, it plainly sounds k, chi, or kappa; as in cable, cobble, cudgel.

Or before the liquids, l and r as in clod and crust.

Or when it ends a former syllabe [sic] before a consonant; as in acquaintance, acknowledgement, action.

In all which it sounds strong.

Before e and i it hath a weak sound, and hisseth like s; as in certain, center, civil, citizen, whence.

Or before the diphthongs: as in cease, deceive.

Among the English-Saxons it obtained the weaker force of chi, or the Italian c; as in capel, canc, cild, cyrce.

Which were pronounced chapel, chance, child, church.

It is sounded with the top of the tongue, striking the upper teeth, and rebounding against the palate.

It is publications like this that allow modern-day linguists and academics to ascertain the way people spoke and how pronunciations changed. Through grammarians in the time of the Tudors and Stuarts,

BEN JONSON'S GRAMMAR

THE
ENGLISH
GRAMMAR.
MADE
BY
BEN. IOHNSON.

For the benefit of all Strangers, out of his obſer-
vation of the Engliſh Language now
ſpoken, and in uſe.

Conſuetudo, certiſſima loquendi Magiſtra, utendumq,
plane ſermone, ut nummo, cui publica
forma eſt. Quinct.

Printed M.DC.XL.

ill 9

but especially Ben Jonson, the language of Shakespeare and what is termed Original Pronunciation, more commonly referred to as OP, can be revived and relived. Through Jonson and others, OP can be recreated with near certainty for certain periods. The reader is told that the R has a doggy sound and would be pronounced with almost a rolling of the tongue, and pronounced hard – perhaps a cross between West Country and Scottish pronunciations today. The demise of the letter H is described, and it can be established that the L was pronounced in words like 'calm'. By piecing it all together it can be said with a great degree of accuracy that Shakespeare's sonnets and poems did actually rhyme, more so than they seem to today. By adopting OP, a lot more of Shakespeare's puns can be readily heard and understood, some of which are quite lewd. It creates a greater understanding of all the plays being written at the time, not just Shakespeare's, and gives a more accurate picture of the language.

Jonson's book also includes the notation of words and parts of speech that were being used during the Jacobean era. Although he was reflecting on language of the day and recording it in the written word, he was also prescriptive as to how things should be in the future. It also included *The Apostrophus* and eight chapters on the syntax of the English language and how one part of speech will relate to another when compiling a sentence.

The whole book was designed not only for English readers but for foreigners learning English as well. Jonson considered that Latin was a universal language and that anyone learning English would already have studied Latin and been quite conversant with the language. Therefore every section of the book was followed by a Latin translation to enable foreigners to grasp the grammar of the English tongue. For the English reader it made the overall book larger than it needed to be, and it was quite tedious having to skip over all the Latin passages. That said, it was another milestone in the history of the English language.

Theatre and plays would change quite dramatically from the Elizabethan era. Most significantly, they shifted from outdoor to indoor venues, and whilst this had some beneficial effects, there were also some disadvantages.

Theatre became a profitable industry during Elizabeth's reign and many innkeepers took advantage and converted their large courtyards into temporary outdoor theatres. These would normally have three tiers of covered balconies with seating around three sides in a circular fashion, with a stage protruding from the fourth side towards the centre of the yard, or pit, which would be standing-room only for the general public, those who could not afford proper seating. They would surround the stage on three sides and became known as 'groundlings', and several hundred would be packed tightly into the pit. The seating areas would be for the more wealthy patrons – the more comfortable the seat and the better the view, the more expensive it was. The plays were very popular among all levels of society, from the poorer working classes to the wealthier merchants, traders, landowners and the aristocracy. The plays would be put on during the afternoon in summer months only because of the lack of artificial lighting. Weather was also an important factor.

At the end of the Elizabethan era and during the first half of the Stuart dynasty, the actual structure of theatres and playhouses changed. The booming entertainment industry proved to be very lucrative for the theatre owners, but was limited to summer months only. Purpose-built indoor theatres started to be erected to enable plays to be performed in the evening as well as all year round. These theatres were a lot smaller than their outdoor predecessors and tended to offer seating without a pit. The ticket prices were a lot more expensive and had the effect of making the theatre exclusive to the rich and therefore well educated sections of society. The ordinary working classes could not afford to attend, thus creating even more of a cultural and educational divide. Many of the rich and wealthy would temporarily convert a large room in their mansion or baronial hall for private theatrical performances for themselves and their guests.

Plays had to be restructured when they were transferred indoors. The only form of lighting available was lots and lots of candles, but these only had a short life span. There had to be more intermissions to light more candles.

Shakespeare continued at his creative best with plays such as *Macbeth* and *The Tempest*. Other playwrights would add to the richness of the English theatre. John Webster, Thomas Middleton and John Ford produced masterpieces, both tragedies and comedies. English theatre would reach its peak during this Jacobean era. Perhaps one of the most significant playwrights of the time other than Shakespeare was Ben Jonson. He had obtained royal patronage and, together with Inigo Jones, helped to create a majesty and an aura around Jacobean theatre, especially with the popularisation of the masque. Inigo Jones was an architect and a skilled stage and costume designer, who created lavish stage settings and outrageous costumes that were integral to the masque. This form of theatrical extravaganza would normally be held privately and reserved exclusively for the royal courts and members of the aristocracy. They usually took the form of a poetical introduction or prologue followed by carefully staged dancing with performers wearing masks. The patrons, who more often than not included royalty, would most probably become involved in the various dancing set pieces, all specifically and expertly choreographed. The masques became self-indulgent performances that underlined the authority and superiority of the nobility and the Divine Right of Kings, and were for the glorification of the royal court generally.

Ben Jonson was the royal favourite and continued to be the court masquer throughout King James's reign, but he was out of favour with Charles I and, as a result, the decline in his popularity gave him time to compile his book on English grammar.

During the reign of Charles I the popularity of the theatre declined somewhat. It had become very expensive to attend and was, generally speaking, for the privileged classes. At the same time the masques became even more extravagant and exclusive. To combat this trend there was a rise in two forms of poetry that prospered greatly at the time. The first was Cavalier poetry, from writers such as Thomas Carew, Richard Lovelace, Robert Herrick and Sir John Suckling. The poems were immensely popular and widely read amongst the educated sector of society. They tended to be easy-to-read celebrations of love, sensuality, comradeship (and King Charles!) and supported living in the moment, *carpe diem* (seize the day), as seen in Robert Herrick's poem, 'To the Virgins, to Make Much of Time'.

Metaphysical poetry was also popular, usually amongst the better-educated members of society. It was highly intellectualised with complex and subtle thoughts, full of paradox and irony. John Donne was probably the central figure of the group of poets loosely defined as 'Metaphysical'. His works have complicated narrative structures and a mixture of subject matter, from playful mistresses on the one hand and confessions asking for repentance on the other. The complex composition was certainly a new kind of challenge to the reader and the listener, who had to concentrate fully.

John Milton, one of England's greatest authors, was emerging during this period. He would make his greatest impact during the time of Oliver Cromwell, but it was in the late Carolean era that he wrote the famous *Areopagitica*, in 1644. This piece has gone down in history as

Gather ye rosebuds while ye may,
Old time is still a-flying:
And this same flower that smiles to-day
To-morrow will be dying.
The glorious lamp of heaven, the sun,
The higher he's a-getting,
The sooner will his race be run,
And nearer he's to setting.
That age is best which is the first,
When youth and blood are warmer;
But being spent, the worse, and worst
Times still succeed the former.
Then be not coy, but use your time,
And while ye may go marry:
For having lost but once your prime
You may for ever tarry.

one of the most eloquent and passionate arguments for the principles of free speech and the freedom of the written word and opposition to censorship. Milton was prominent during the Commonwealth, but it was during the Restoration that he finished his epic poem *Paradise Lost*, the biblical story of the Fall of Man, the temptation of Adam and Eve and their expulsion from the Garden of Eden. It is recognised as one of the great works written in the English language.

Science was also making great strides through the Stuart era both before the Commonwealth and afterwards. Francis Bacon was the leading light and is recognised as laying the foundations for scientific observation and recording. Many scientific scholars were influenced by Bacon and through their work many new scientific words started to enter the English language, some of which were included in Thomas Blount's dictionary *Glossographia*. Bacon would be one of the founding members of the Royal Society in the reign of Charles II. One of the early presidents was the diarist Samuel Pepys, and one of the earliest scientists to join the society was Isaac Newton, who made discoveries in several fields of science and mathematics, especially with his laws of universal gravitation.

International exploration, colonisation and trade continued under the Stuarts, especially in North America. Jamestown, Virginia, was founded in 1607 by the Charter of the Virginia Company of London, also known as the Virginia Company, which was a joint stock company with the sole purpose of establishing colonial settlements in North America. It was established by royal charter in 1606 by James I, thus Jamestown bears his name. In 1610 the Society of Merchant Venturers founded a permanent settlement in Cuper's Cove in Newfoundland. Two years later Saint George's on the island of Bermuda was founded and established.

In 1620 the most famous British colonial settlement was established when the Pilgrim Fathers set sail from Plymouth, England on the *Mayflower* and founded *New Plimouth* in Massachusetts. These pilgrims were members of the English Separatist Church, a strict branch of Puritanism who wanted to set up a religious community in the New World based on their Puritan beliefs. They disagreed with the religious settlement of the Church of England, believing it to be a compromise between Roman Catholicism and Protestantism. They were opposed to King James's attitude towards religion and objected to his version of the Bible and compulsory use of *The Book of Common Prayer* in church services. They remained defiant and continued to attend their own Puritan meetings, for which they were persecuted. Some escaped to the Netherlands and some boarded the *Mayflower* to start afresh in the New World – others would soon follow.

More British colonies were established, firstly in 1634 in Maryland, so called because two years previously King Charles I insisted that the new acquisition was to be named in honour of his wife, Queen Mary. Within two years Connecticut and Rhode Island were acquired, the former being named from the Native American word *quinnehtukqut*, meaning a tidal river.

During the Civil War in England and the Commonwealth that followed there was a subsequent decline in colonisation. However, during the Restoration overseas activity increased and the New Netherlands was acquired from the Dutch and renamed the Province of New York. More territory would be acquired and England became the major power in North America.

More words from Native Americans would be adopted into the English vocabulary, this time through more direct contact rather than through Spanish or Portuguese, as had previously happened with the Elizabethan privateers.

Whilst the three English civil wars between the Parliamentarians and those loyal to the king were taking place, and during the Commonwealth that followed, many things were put on hold. Harsh Puritan laws were passed by Oliver Cromwell, which included the theatre being banned, only to return during Charles II's reign with bawdy Restoration comedy that would include female actors. Dancing round the maypole was forbidden and all sports banned; boys caught playing football on a Sunday were to be whipped. Many inns and taverns were closed, and women caught doing certain chores on a Sunday would be put in the stocks, among many other such draconian measures. One of these so-called reforms did have an effect on the English language: all court proceedings were to be conducted and spoken in English, a move that upset the legal profession at the time.

There was a decline in international trade as well as overseas colonisation whilst Cromwell increased his military campaigns in Ireland and Scotland. But, once the restoration of the monarchy began in 1660, many of Cromwell's reforms were rescinded and things started to move again. International exploration and trade continued to grow, not only in America and the Caribbean but in Africa, India and as far afield as China. In a series of five acts, King Charles II granted the English East India Company the rights practically to monopolise

English Words adopted direct from Native American

English word	Native American word	translation
caribou	qalipu	snow shoveller
chipmunk	chitmunk	red squirrel
Eskimo	aiachkimeou	snow shoe netter
hickory	hiquara	hard wood tree
husky	huskemaw	Eskimo dog
igloo	iglu	house
kayak	qajaq	canoe
moccasin	mockasin	shoe
moose	moos (several variations)	strips off
nanook	nanuq	polar bear
opossum	apasum	white dog
papoose	pappouse	baby
pecan	pakan	nut
persimmon	pessemin	fruit – berry
pow wow	powwaw	to dream
raccoon	aroughcun	rubs and scratches with its hands
skunk	squnck	urinating fox
squash	askutasquash	fruit
squaw	squa	wife
terrapin	torope	turtle
toboggan	topaqan	sled
tomahawk	tamahaac	cutting tool
totem	nin doodem	my spiritual emblem
wigwam	wiigiwaam	their house

Fig 44

Some English words adopted indirectly from Native Caribbean and American peoples, via Spanish, Portuguese and French

English word	original word	English word	original word
alpaca	allpaka	avocado	ahuacati
barbecue	barbakoa	bayou	bayuk
cacoa / cocoa	cacua	canoe	canaoua
cannibal	kanpona	cashew	caju
cayenne	kyynha	chili	chilli
chocolate	chocalati	condor	kuntur
cougar	guacuarana	coyote	coyoti
coypu	koypu	guacamole	ahuacamolli
guano	huano	hammock	hamaka
hooch	Hoochinoo	hurricane	hurakan
iguana	iwana	Inca	Inca
jaguar	yaguara	jerky	charki
llama	lama	macaw	macavuana
maize	mahis	maraca	maraka
ocelot	tiati-oceloti	pampas	pampa
piranha	pira sainha	potato	batata
puma	puma	quinine	kinakina
savann	zabana	shack	xahcalli
tapioca	tipioca	tapir	tapyra
tomato	tomati	toucan	tucan

Fig 45

Examples of some words adopted into English Language through trade, commerce and exploration 1600AD to 1900AD

Modern English	source	when	Modern English	source	when
algorithm	Arabic al-Kwarizmi	late C17th	amok	Malay amok Portuguese amouco	mid C17th
balcony	Italian balcone	early C17th	ballet	Italian balleto	mid C17th
bizarre	Italian bizzaro	mid C17th	brigade	Italian brigata	mid C17th
caddy	Malay kati	late C18th	chocolate	Spanish via Aztec chocolati	early C17th
detail	French détail	early C17th	fetish	Portuguese feitiço	early C17th
geisha	Japanese gei sha	late C19th	geyser	Icelandic geysir	late C18th
gong	Malay gong	early C17th	grotto	Greek via Italian grotta	early C17th
harem	Arabic harama	mid C17th	ketchup	Chinese k'e chap	late C17th
kiosk	Turkish kóşk via French kiosque	early C17th	kowtow	Chinese kētō	early C19th
mammoth	Siberian mamont	early C18th	opera	Italian opera	mid C17th
prestige	Latin via French presige	mid C17th	rocket	Italian roochetto via French roquette	early C17th
saga	Old Norse saga	early C18th	salon	French salon	late C17th
samurai	Japanese samurai	mid C19th	sauna	Finnish sauna	late C19th
shawl	Persian śäl	early C17th	sherbet	Arabic sariba via Turkish serbet	early C17th
ski	Old Norse skith	mid C18th	tank	Sanskrit via Portuguese tangue	early C17th
taboo	Tongan tabu	late C18th	tea	Chinese te	mid C17th
troll	Old Norse troll	mid C19th	tycoon	Japanese taikun	mid C19th

Fig 46

the East. They could acquire land as and when they saw fit, had the authority to print money, form political and trading alliances with whomever they thought would be beneficial to the Crown and England, administer justice where they deemed it necessary and other similar powers to enable them to dominate the Indian subcontinent and further east.

This overall increase in overseas activity would eventually lay the foundations for further expansion and the building of an empire in subsequent centuries. With these new developments, more and more words were being adopted into the English language.

The hunt for exotic spices from further afield than the subcontinent in order to satisfy an ever growing demand in England, to say nothing of the commercial desire to have a bigger say in the lucrative global spice trade, meant that English ships were now sailing into previously uncharted waters and coming into conflict with other nations doing the same – especially the Dutch.

12

The Dutch and Flemish

During the Commonwealth period and the Restoration, the English were engaged in three naval conflicts against the Netherlands, known as the Anglo-Dutch Wars. Both were trying to become the eminent sea power in Europe and foremost in overseas exploration and trade. The Dutch had built up the largest mercantile fleet in Europe and had established a near monopoly in the Indonesian spice trade by defeating the Portuguese, the only other nation extensively involved in this trade. The Dutch had also established settlements in both the East and the West, with colonies in North America and trading routes with the Dutch East India Company in Indonesia. To accomplish this they had also built up a large naval fleet with modern ships and well-trained men. Their fishing fleet was also encroaching into waters considered to be under English jurisdiction.

The overall effect was that the Dutch fleets controlled the English Channel, the North Sea and routes to the East Indies. England wanted to rule the waves and increase its colonies in foreign climes. A conflict therefore arose between the two countries and resulted in three fairly uninspiring conflicts between 1652 and 1674. The overall outcome was that the Dutch controlled the spice trade and established a monopoly over nutmeg, whilst England gained Dutch territories in North America.

The Dutch, however, had not always been the enemy – quite the reverse, in fact. Throughout history the Dutch and the Dutch-speaking Flemings had regularly been invited over to England to assist in certain industries, such as the wool and cloth trades and land reclamation. They were considered to be more advanced and more highly skilled in whichever trade or industry they were being invited over to join – sometimes with encouragement from the English monarch at the time.

Other than the Frisians, who came over with the Angles, the next big influx was the Flemish army with William I in 1066. Flemish communities tended to centre round Norman castle towns and very soon afterwards set up a weaving industry on the island. Associated trades grew alongside the weaving trade, and soon they had all become integrated into an English way of life. In 1270 Henry III realised the wool trade in Flanders was undergoing some difficulties and he encouraged Flemish weavers to leave Flanders and to put a new impetus into the industry in England. Later, in 1331, Edward III encouraged more Dutch weavers to England to help in the ever-growing English wool trade.

During the sixteenth and seventeenth centuries there were several waves of Dutch and Flemish migration to England. There was religious unrest in parts of the Low Countries, which were under the control of either the Spanish or the French at this time, both staunchly Roman Catholic nations. A great number of Dutch and Flemish Protestants were escaping from persecution and travelled to England for refuge. These were normally skilled artisans such as gunsmiths, printers, glaziers, tapestry makers, felt makers, knife makers and others who were making a new life in England. Dutch engineers were engaged in many land drainage and irrigation schemes throughout England and responsible for land reclamation in the Fens.

During the time of the English Renaissance, Dutch masters were celebrated as the biggest influence in the world of visual art, and many Dutch portrait and landscape painters were employed, some with royal patronage.

Eventually, the Dutch and Flemish would be instrumental in developing the cotton industry in Manchester and the steel industry in Newcastle; they introduced knife-making in Sheffield, started a felt-hat industry, made cables, ropes and hawsers for the English Navy, introduced the manufacture of paper, and much more.

Many everyday words in the English vocabulary have been adopted from the Dutch and Flemish.

Examples of some English words adopted from the Dutch & Flemish

English	Dutch	English	Dutch	English	Dutch
avast	hou'vast	beleaguer	belegeren	blare	blaren
blink	blinken	bluff (deceive)	bluffen	blunderbus	donderbus
boodle	boedel	boom	boom	booze	būsen
boss	baas	brackish	brac	brandy	brandewijn
brick	bricke	buoy	boye	bumkin	bommekijn
bundle	bundel	bung	bonghe	coffee	koffie
coleslaw	koolsla	cramp	krampe	crap	krappe
cruise	kruis	curl	krul	dam	dam
dapper	dapper	deck	dekken	decoy	de kouw
dock	dok	dredge	dregghe	drill	drillen
easel	ezel	etch	etsen	foist	vuist
forlorn hope	verloren hoop	freight	vrecht	frolic	vrolijk
gherkin	gurhje	gimp	gimp	golf	kolf
grab	grabben	gruff	grof	hanker	hunkeren
hoist	hijsen	holster	holster	iceberg	ijsberg
jib	giiben	keelhaul	kielhalen	knapsack	knapzack
landscape	lantscap	leak	lek	loiter	loteren
lottery	loterij	luck	lucken	maelstrom	maalenstroom
manikin	manneken	mart	marct	measels	masel
mumps	mompen	offal	afval	onslaught	aenslag
pickle	pekel	plug	plugge	polder	polre
poppycock	pappekak	pump	pomp	reef	rif / ref

Fig 47 |

Examples of some English words adopted from the Dutch & Flemish

English	Dutch	English	Dutch	English	Dutch
roster	rooster	rover	roven	school (of fish)	schole
schooner	schoener	scone	schoonbroot (fine bread)	scum	schūm
shoal	schole	sketch	schets	skipper	schipper
sleigh	slei	sloop	sloep	slurp	slurpen
smelt	smelten	smuggle	smuggeln	snack	snacken
snoop	snœpen	spook	spook	spool	spoel
splinter	splenter	split	splitten	stoker	stoken
stripe	strippen	tattoo	taptoe	trigger	trekken
wiggle	wigglen	yacht	jaghtschip (fast pirate ship)		

Fig 47 II

13

The Georgian and Victorian Eras

The Georgian era and the subsequent Victorian age are hugely important in the evolution of the English language, both in the written form and the spoken word. The building of an empire that stretched around the world, an agrarian and ensuing industrial revolution, great strides in scientific discovery and an explosion in printed English literature in books, pamphlets and newspapers would all have a massive effect on the English language and bring about the introduction of even more words into the English vocabulary.

Finally, a Standard English would unofficially emerge that was accepted by academics and educationalists alike and have a far wider range than the London–Cambridge–Oxford triangle. It would have a more universal acceptance, especially in the middle and upper classes of English society, and would also be introduced into the education system at the time.

However, at the beginning of the period a standardised version of the language did not seem possible. In the last two years of Queen Anne's reign, prior to the Georgian era, Jonathan Swift, the Anglo-Irish author of *Gulliver's Travels* and other classics, wrote to the Earl of Oxford about the chaotic and inconsistent English language. It took the form of a manuscript and was entitled *Proposal for Correcting, Improving and Ascertaining the English Tongue*, in which the second paragraph states:

[2] My Lord; I do here in the Name of all the Learned and Polite Persons of the Nation, complain to your LORDSHIP, as *First Minister,* that our Language is extremely imperfect; that its

daily Improvements are by no means in proportion to its daily Corruptions; and the Pretenders to polish and refine it, have chiefly multiplied Abuses and Absurdities; and, that in many Instances, it offends against every Part of Grammar. But lest Your LORDSHIP should think my Censure to be too severe, I shall take leave to be more particular.

Swift gained the support of a number of writers and authors, including Daniel Defoe, Joseph Addison and Alexander Pope. They called for the introduction of an Academy of the English Language to create standards in spelling and grammar. They were trying to achieve something in the mould of the *Académie Française* and its formalising of the French language. Whilst the idea had support from Queen Anne, it was fiercely contested by others and petered out after Anne's death.

Many dictionaries, books on pronunciation and books on spelling and grammar were printed in the eighteenth and nineteenth centuries, which exacerbated the problem of creating any form of standard. There were so many inconsistencies in these publications that they highlighted the differences rather than creating a uniform set of linguistic rules. Despite these inconsistencies, a small group of scholars would shine above all the others, working independently of one another to help shape a standard in English by the end of the 1700s that would be actively encouraged throughout the 1800s; so successful, in fact, that it would become even more elitist than Chancery English, and regional dialects would thereafter be looked down upon with scorn and distaste.

Early dictionaries had tended to give definitions to the harder words in the language rather than all of the words in the English vocabulary. The first dictionary to encompass all known words in the English language was published in 1721 and compiled by Nathaniel Bailey, entitled *An Universal Etymological English Dictionary*. It became one of the most popular dictionaries in the 1700s, with thirty editions printed by the early 1800s and sales far outstripping most other dictionaries of the time. It was more than 900 pages long with over 60,000 definitions. In his task of compiling the text, Bailey was greatly influenced by two previous dictionaries, John Kersey's *Dictionarium Anglo-Britannicum,* which appeared in 1706, and Edward Phillips' *The New World of English Words,* published at the end of the 1600s. Ironically, despite its immense popularity

SWIFT'S PROPOSAL ON GRAMMAR

A
PROPOSAL
FOR
Correcting, Improving and *Afcertaining*
THE
𝕰𝖓𝖌𝖑𝖎𝖘𝖍 𝕿𝖔𝖓𝖌𝖚𝖊;
IN A
LETTER
To the Most Honourable
ROBERT
Earl *of* Oxford *and* Mortimer,
Lord High Treaſurer
OF
GREAT BRITAIN.

LONDON:
Printed for BEN J. TOOKE, at the
Middle-Temple-Gate, Fleet Street, 1712

ill 10

Bailey's *An Universal Etymological English Dictionary* was not the most influential dictionary and had little effect on helping to establish a standardised English.

The inconsistencies in spelling and grammar in all the English dictionaries, as well as in all other forms of printed material such as books, magazines and pamphlets, etc., led to great dissatisfaction amongst the ever-increasing numbers of the population who could read. In 1746 a group of London businessmen saw an opportunity and a niche in the market. They contracted Samuel Johnson to compile a dictionary and paid him the sum of £1,575 for the task.

Samuel Johnson was the son of a Lichfield bookseller and from birth was surrounded by books. He was well educated, although lack of funds curtailed his studies at Oxford University. His career was varied: he was a teacher, poet, literary critic, biographer, editor, columnist and lexicographer. It was the latter for which he became most famous and, in this work he has had an everlasting effect on the English language.

Johnson was writing for a publication called *The Gentleman's Magazine* when he was approached by a group of booksellers and publishers. After negotiations, Johnson agreed to create an English dictionary that he hoped would bring some consistency to a hitherto untamed and chaotic language. The timescale agreed for research and compiling this epic work was three years, and Johnson was paid 1,500 guineas (£1,575). Three years seemed very ambitious for just one man and a clerical assistant – and so it proved. Johnson in fact took nine years of meticulous research, referencing and cross-referencing and creating innovative literary illustrations. During Johnson's preparation he published a *Plan of a Dictionary of the English Language*, which described how he was going to undertake this momentous task. In it is a very telling passage that perhaps explains why the eventual dictionary became so highly regarded and was such an iconic step in the history of the English language:

> I shall therefore, since the rules of stile, like those of law, arise from precedents often repeated, collect the testimonies of both sides, and endeavour to discover and promulgate the decrees of custom, who has so long possessed whether by right or by usurpation, the sovereignty of words.

Johnson was able to read and recite *The Book of Common Prayer* at the tender age of four and had been taught Latin in his later

SAMUEL JOHNSON'S BOOK ON GRAMMAR

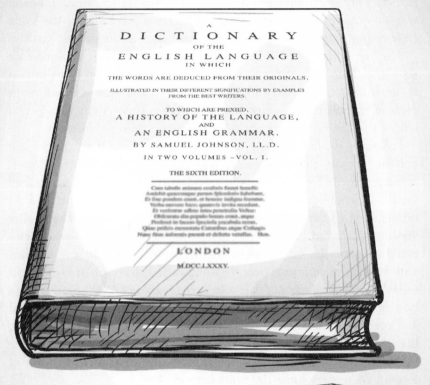

A

D I C T I O N A R Y

OF THE

ENGLISH LANGUAGE

IN WHICH

THE WORDS ARE DEDUCED FROM THEIR ORIGINALS,

ILLUSTRATED IN THEIR DIFFERENT SIGNIFICATIONS BY EXAMPLES
FROM THE BEST WRITERS.

TO WHICH ARE PREXIED,

A HISTORY OF THE LANGUAGE,

AND

AN ENGLISH GRAMMAR.

BY SAMUEL JOHNSON, LL.D.

IN TWO VOLUMES – VOL. I.

THE SIXTH EDITION.

LONDON

M.DCC.LXXXV.

ill 11

schooling. Through his varied literary career he was also surrounded with books and manuscripts containing the more unstructured language of authors, poets and playwrights such as Shakespeare and the like. In other words, he was going to compare words and phrases that he considered proper and right alongside their corrupted variations. Dependent on the most common usage, Johnson would then make a decision as to which one he thought was correct and record accordingly. He was effectively standardising the language and backing it up with examples and literary illustrations. Johnson was unique in that he was being both prescriptive and at the same time responding to common descriptive usage: a remarkable quality.

The first edition, in 1755, was a huge construction. It was one foot six inches high and even wider by some two inches, and came in two volumes containing nearly 43,000 definitions. It truly was a mammoth printing problem: no other book this size, other than the special editions of the Bible in earlier times, had ever been published.

Following the first edition, *Johnson's Dictionary*, as it was to become known, or just the *Dictionary*, was issued in a number of ways. It featured in 165 weekly parts in a fashionable magazine. An abridged version was published in 1756 in a considerably cheaper version than the original first edition, which at £4 10s 0 was very expensive. The smaller version became so popular that it sold in excess of a thousand copies every year for the next three decades. The original had five editions with various amendments over the same period, and even at the price in today's terms of nearly £650, it sold in the region of 6,000 copies; that's how important the *Dictionary* had become. It was very much respected and revered throughout the land and further afield. More importantly, it had set a standard for others to follow and remained the foremost authority well after Johnson's death, until the introduction of the *Oxford English Dictionary* some 100 years later in 1884.

Another development was taking place during the same period as Johnson's huge task that would also have a lasting effect well into the next century and beyond. A great number of books were now being written on English grammar, more so than at any other time previously. Approximately 200 books were written on English grammar in the second half of the eighteenth century, and close on 800 were written during the nineteenth. But two grammarians would stand above the rest and have an influence well into the twentieth century. The first grammarian was Robert Lowth, a Church of England Bishop of London and a professor of poetry at Oxford, well versed in Latin and the classics. After he had completed his treatise on Hebrew

poetry he turned his efforts to writing *A Short Introduction to English Grammar*, which was published in 1762. It became very popular with an ever-increasing middle class in England searching for the correct use of the language. It was reissued no less than forty-five times by the end of 1790s. The book was authoritative and prescriptive in its approach; it served very much like a textbook for adults and was much too difficult for schoolchildren, but it appealed to the more educated classes of society. Lowth applied many Latin principles to the Germanic-based English language in an attempt to lend the authority of an ancient language to the motley modern tongue.

It was Lowth who prescribed strict rules on grammar that would be emulated by other grammarians. He decided that sentences should not end with a preposition, and that the splitting of an infinitive, such as 'to slowly turn the dial', or 'to gradually add the ingredients', are grammatically incorrect. Lowth's *A Short Introduction to English Grammar* would become the basis for a standardised English grammar.

Despite Lowth's popularity, it would be an American Quaker immigrating to Yorkshire who would produce the most popular book on this subject. Lindley Murray published *English Grammar Adapted to the Different Class of Learners* in 1795. The book was written in response to a local Friends' School asking him to create an easy-to-read textbook on English grammar. Perhaps Murray looked at several existing books on the subject, but it was surely Lowth's *A Short Introduction to English Grammar* that he used as the starting point, which Murray basically simplified. His intention to create a simple handbook on grammar was spelt out in the book's introduction:

> When the number and variety of English Grammars already, and the ability with which some of them are written, are considered, little can be expected from a new compilation, besides a careful selection of the most useful matter, and some degree of improvement in the mode of adapting it to the understanding, and the gradual process of learners.

Murray's book was immensely popular, especially in schools, and widely adopted in the education boom that was to occur in the 1800s with the introduction of state education. Murray's book would be reissued no less than 200 times by the mid-1800s, selling over 20,000,000 copies. It was translated into many languages and was also extremely popular in the burgeoning English-speaking United

LOWTH'S BOOK
ON GRAMMAR

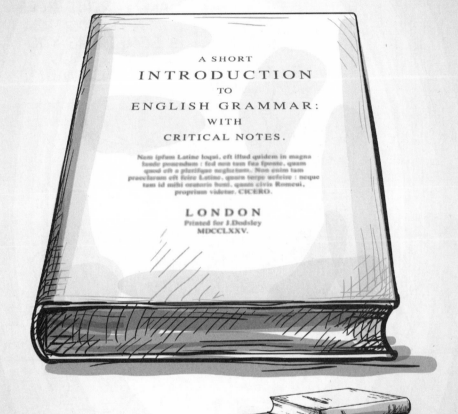

A SHORT

INTRODUCTION

TO

ENGLISH GRAMMAR:

WITH

CRITICAL NOTES.

Nam ipfum Latine loqui, eft illud quidem in magna
laude ponendum : fed non tam fua fponte, quam
quod eft a plerifque neglectum. Non enim tam
praeclarum eft fcire Latine, quam turpe nefcire : neque
tam id mihi oratoris boni, quam civis Romeui,
proprium videtur. CICERO.

LONDON
Printed for J.Dodsley
MDCCLXXV.

ill 12

States of America. It would continue in popularity and become the basis for subsequent handbooks and textbooks on grammar, up to and including post-war Britain in the 1940s and '50s.

Standards had started to become established in English in both spelling and grammar by the late 1700s. There had also evolved a standard in speech and pronunciation, especially amongst the more literate middle and upper classes, albeit with slight regional differences. There was, however, still a missing link.

Thus far an unofficial standard in pronunciation had evolved from the London–Cambridge–Oxford triangle, with some influences from the more densely populated and wealthy East Midlands. The ever-growing middle classes felt in desperate need of correct grammar, spelling and pronunciation. Johnson and Lowth had catered for the first two needs with their publications in 1775 and 1762 respectively. The timing was perfect for a similar authoritative work on regulating pronunciation, rhetoric and public speaking. Thomas Sheridan was the answer. He was educated at Westminster School during the 1730s and returned to his native Ireland to obtain a BA and a subsequent MA at Dublin University. Eventually he returned to England and published *A Course of Lectures on Elocution* at just the right time to coincide with Johnson and Lowth. Sheridan's book was so popular that elocution and pronunciation became established in both public schools and private education. The book was so fashionable that there were a number of American editions as well.

It is reasonable to deduce that from the merging of Johnson's dictionary, Lowth's grammar and Sheridan's instruction on pronunciation and elocution, a Standard English as we know it today started to emerge. Further, at the beginning of the 1800s it is also reasonable to assume that because Johnson, Murray and Sheridan were popular in America, English and American English were more alike then than at any other time.

By the early 1800s standards had become established in all aspects of the English language. In the main, those standard were only maintained by the educated middle and upper classes who could afford to have a decent education, purchase magazines and books – including the likes of a *Johnson Dictionary* – and be at ease with public speaking and debate. However, there were still slight regional variations. Standard English had become very elitist and there was a great divide between the educated and uneducated. The distinct regional dialects, spoken by the vast majority of the population, were frowned upon and ridiculed by many writers of the day. This can be readily demonstrated in the introduction of a dictionary

entitled *Vocabulary of East Anglia* compiled by the Reverend Forby and printed in 1830. After several years of research the book was complete, all bar the aforementioned introduction. Unfortunately, the Revd Forby died and a friend wrote the opening chapter, which provides a classic example of the elitist attitude towards a provincial dialect (see page 220).

Despite the presence of this new standardised English, there was still a dispute amongst learned and academic scholars over the controversial letter H. As already described in a previous chapter, the letter H as an initial letter was mor or less dropped by the time of Shakespeare, and in *Richard III* the principal player would be calling for his *'orse*. This dispute over the pronunciation of the letter H had not only continued throughout the reign of the Stuarts but also through the Georgian and Victorian eras, and is still not fully resolved in the present day.

Ben Jonson, in his *English Grammar* (1640), puts H as the last letter of the alphabet and questions if it is a letter at all: 'Whether a letter or no ... but be it a letter, or spirit, we have great use of it in our tongue, both before and after vowels.' Just over 100 years later Samuel Johnson's dictionary states that the letter H is 'sounded only by a strong emission of breath, without any conformation of the organs of speech, and is therefore by many grammarians accounted no letter'.

The argument over the pronunciation or non-pronunciation of the letter H carried on for another 100 years, and in 1854 a book was published entitled *The Poor Letter H Its Use and Abuse*, written by The Hon. Henry H. In it he states:

H IS ALWAYS TO BE SOUNDED AT THE BEGINNING OF WORDS, except the following, and all the words that are produced from them:

SPELLED	PRONOUNCED
Heir, Heiress	Eir, Eiress.
Honest, Honesty	Onest, Onesty.
Honour, Honourable	Onour, Onourable.
Herb, Herbage	Erb, Erbage.
Hospital	Ospital.
Hostler	Ostler.
Hour	Our.
Humour, Humourous	Umour, Umourous.

Some folks say that humble and humility should be included in this list, and I think so too.

Vocabulary of East Anglia

by Rev. Robert Forby published 1830AD

Excerpt from the 'Introduction'

From a writer who offers to the public a volume on a *Provincial Dialect*, and ventures to announce his intention of confirming, by *authority* and etymology, the strange words and phrases he is about to produce, some introductory explanation of his design may reasonably be required. The very mention of such an undertaking is likely to be received with ridicule, contempt, or even disgust ; as if little or nothing more could be expected, than from analysing the rude jargon of some semi-barbarous tribe ; as if, being merely oral, and existing only among the unlettered rustic vulgar of a particular district, *Provincial Language* were of little concern to general readers, of still less to persons of refined education, and much below the notice of philologists.

However justly this censure may be pronounced on a fabricated farrago of cant, slang, or what has more recently been denominated *flash language*, spoken by vagabonds, mendicants, and outcasts ; by sharpers, swindlers, and felons ; for the better concealment of their illegal practices, and for their more effectual separation from the "good men and true" of regular and decent society ; it certainly is by no means applicable to any form whatsoever of a *National Language*, constituting the vernacular tongue of any province of that nation. Such forms, be they as many and as various as they may, are all, in substance, remnants and derivatives of the language of past ages, which were, at some time or other, in common use, though in long process of time they have become only locally used and understood.

…...On this principle, two dictionaries might be constructed, perfectly separate, but of concurrent authority and utility. One would contain all that is necessary for the various purposes of Science and Literature. The other a complete digest of the vulgar and colloquial tongue. In one or the other, fit reception would be provided for every known word, properly English, with the total exclusion of all cant, slang, and flash; for which the proper place is one, of which the author has often heard, but never saw – the Scoundrel's Dictionary.

Should any reader expect to find under this title, rules by which he may learn to speak East Anglian, he will be disappointed. No such attempt was intended. If the coarse cacophonies of unlettered boors were of any interest to philologists, the attempt would be nugatory. . . ..…...

Fig 48

POOR LETTER H
ITS USE AND ABUSE

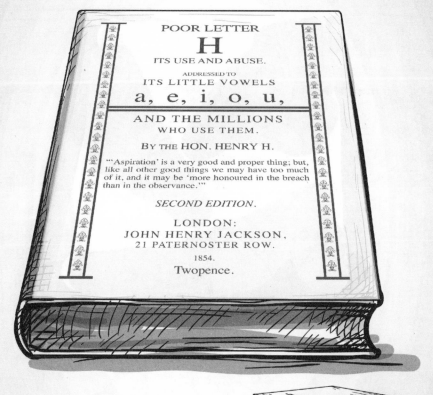

POOR LETTER

H

ITS USE AND ABUSE.

ADDRESSED TO

ITS LITTLE VOWELS

a, e, i, o, u,

AND THE MILLIONS
WHO USE THEM.

BY THE HON. HENRY H.

"'Aspiration' is a very good and proper thing; but, like all other good things we may have too much of it, and it may be 'more honoured in the breach than in the observance.'"

SECOND EDITION.

LONDON:
JOHN HENRY JACKSON,
21 PATERNOSTER ROW.
1854.
Twopence.

ill 13

In 1857 *Harry Hawkin's H book; shewing how he learned to aspirate his H's* was published, but its author remained anonymous. Although quite popular, it was surpassed in 1880 by a book entitled *The Letter H, Past, Present, and Future* by Alfred Leach. This latter attempt was to try and finally establish the proper use of this unfortunate letter and was subtitled *A Treatise, With Rules for the Silent H, Based on Modern Usage, and Notes on Wh*. A simple quote from this publication highlights the plight of the H and the arguments and controversies it had caused:

> On no point of English pronunciation have authorities more notoriously disagreed than that of words beginning with H; and if any one wishes to see the fathers of English Orthoepy at loggerheads, or the Doctors of Modern English Pronunciation in a muddle, let them glance at the H section of their various dictionaries.

The discussions and arguments continued not only on its pronunciation, but also what article should precede it. It should be 'an historic event' not 'a historic event', although it is 'a history lesson' and not 'an history lesson'; but it can be either 'a hotel' or 'an 'otel' and even 'an hotel'. The discussions are still ongoing.

One strange outcome from this continuing controversy was the actual pronunciation of the letter 'H' itself. From Tudor times to the Victorians there had of course been religious turmoil, sometimes very violent, between Protestants and Catholics. It would appear that somewhere along the line, the letter H took on two different pronunciations that correlated with this religious divide: the Protestants would pronounce the letter H as 'aitch' and the Catholics would pronounce it as 'haitch'. The latter has its roots with the Norman-French word *hache* describing the lower case h as a 'hatchet'.

It would appear that where there were Catholic strongholds in England, the 'haitch' became predominant in dialectal English, for example as in East London, parts of Yorkshire and likewise Lancashire. The Republic of Ireland pronounces it as 'haitch' whereas in Northern Ireland its pronunciation reflects the Protestant/Catholic split. The Roman Catholic Church had a big influence in the education system in Australia, and that is why 60 per cent of Australians say 'haitch'. The reason for hearing some presenters and commentators on television and radio now saying 'haitch' instead of 'aitch' is that more and more presenters have regional dialects and not the BBC English favoured in days past. The debate continues.

During the 1700s and 1800s colonialism was an important element in the fabric of English society, so much so that by the end of the nineteenth century the British Empire would stretch around the world with more than a foothold in every continent. It was said that the sun never set on the British Empire. The extent of colonisation, as Britain secured and annexed her overseas territories, would gradually increase in two major waves, usually after very violent and bloody battles.

The so-called First British Empire would expand from small territorial gains in the Elizabethan era to wide-reaching domains during the Georgian dynasty. Thirteen American colonies had been established along with territories in Canada, and expansion in India had taken place with all other European rivals having been physically deterred. International trade increased dramatically with more trading companies, trading posts and trading routes being established. Some of the most lucrative and profitable trades that England dominated were the tobacco industry in Virginia, the barbaric slave trade between African states, the Caribbean and the American colonies, the tea trade from China and India, and the export of plant and machinery during the height of the Industrial Revolution. England also maintained its position as 'Ruler of the Waves' with her Royal Navy as well as the mercantile fleet. However in 1783, during the reign of George III, the thirteen American colonies rebelled and gained independence from the British with victory in the American War of Independence. This is seen by many historians as the end of the First British Empire.

Thereafter the remaining British colonies were enlarged and new colonies were founded, settled and exploited. The Second British Empire was about to expand to become the largest empire the world had ever seen. Australia and New Zealand became important parts of the Empire and large swathes of territory in Africa, from the Mediterranean coast to the tip of South Africa, would come under British rule. The Victorian era is seen as the height of the British Empire, encompassing one quarter of the world's land mass and controlling hundreds of millions of different peoples throughout the world.

The English language would be greatly affected by this expansion, with words being adopted into the vocabulary from the indigenous peoples living in the British colonies around the world, and also new words introduced via the expansion of international trade outside the empire.

Some of the words adopted into English from other languages during England's empire building and colonialism

From India, Pakistan, Bangladesh and Sri Lanka

bandanna · bamboo · bangle · bungalow · catamaran · cheetah · cheroot
chit · chutney · cot · cummerbund · curry · cushy · dinghy
dungarees · gymkhana · jodhpurs · juggernaut · jungle · khaki · karma
loot · mongoose · mulligatawny · pukka · punch (the drink) · pundit
pyjamas · shampoo · thug · toddy · typhoon · veranda · yoga

From Australia, New Zealand and parts of Polynesia

budgerigar · billabong · boomerang · didgeridoo · dingo · haka · kangaroo
kia ora · kiwi · koala · taboo · tattoo · kookaburra · wallaby · wombat

From parts of Africa including Egypt and South Africa

aardvark · Afrikaans · apartheid · banjo · biltong · Boer · chemistry
chimpanzee · ebony · eland · gnu · ibis · jumbo · meerkat
mummi · oasis · obelisk · Pharaoh · pyramid · rooibos · safari
sphinx · springbok · trek · tsetse · wildebeest · zebra · zombie

From Republic of Ireland, Scotland, Northern Ireland and Wales

banshee · bard · bog · brogue · brogues · caber · cairn · capercaillie
ceilidh · clan · claymore · colleen · coracle · corgi · corrie · crag
eisteddfod · galore · gillie · gob · hooligan · kerfuffle · leprechaun
limmerick · loch · penguin · plaid · poteen · ptarmigan · shamrock
shindig · slogan · sporran · smithereens · Tory · trousers · whisky(ey)

Fig 49

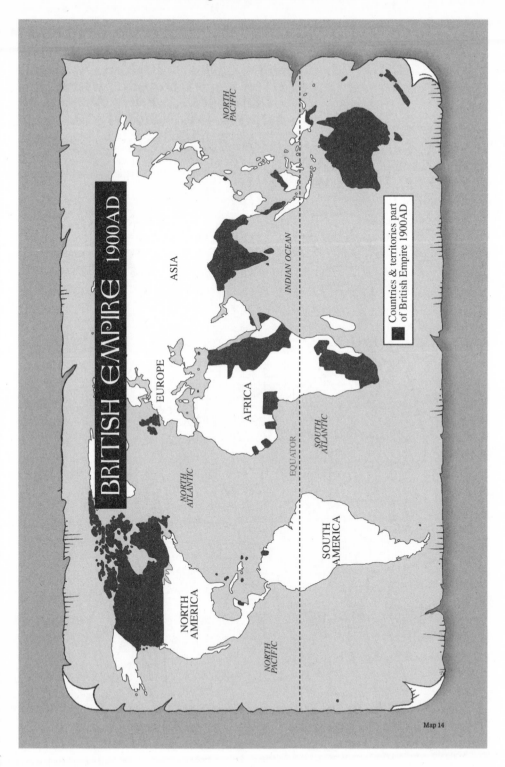

BRITISH EMPIRE 1900AD

Countries & territories part
of British Empire 1900AD

Map 14

During the eighteenth and nineteenth centuries England saw a massive population explosion, and the advance of mechanisation in the Agrarian Revolution was quickly followed by the Industrial Revolution.

The height of the Agrarian Revolution, often called the Agricultural Revolution, saw a meteoric rise in food production, which helped to sustain the dramatic increase in population. Within 100 years from 1700 the population of England nearly doubled, from just under 5,000,000 to nearly 9,000,000. Other population booms had occurred before in history but the head count quickly declined again, either because food production could not cope and people died of starvation or outbreaks of the plague would drastically decrease the numbers. One particular innovation was a change in farming methods from the centuries-old three-field crop rotation system. One field would have a cereal crop whilst the next one would have peas, lentils or beans; the third field was left fallow to enable it to recover, at the same time having animals set to pasture to naturally fertilise the soil. Each year the system would rotate, so each field went through a three-year cycle.

The technique that replaced it was a four-field system expanded to include root crops such as turnips in the winter in order to utilise the different nutrients deeper in the soil. It also included the planting of clover as animal fodder, which had the added bonus of being a green manure when ploughed back in. Not only did the new system virtually double the output of crops per acre, it produced more fodder for the increase in livestock needed to feed the rise in population.

The Agrarian Revolution was so called because it also saw sweeping changes through mechanisation. Names like Jethro Tull, James Ransome, James Smyth, William Sims, John Jeffries and others are synonymous with agricultural inventions that changed the world of farming. English manufacturers of agricultural machinery, such as Garrett's of Leiston, would become the leaders in world exports.

With agriculture becoming more industrialised, many new words and phrases entered the English vocabulary. Some words and terms were part of the terminology of these new machines and techniques, such as 'horse hoe', 'lever corn drill', 'horsepower', 'steam threshing machine', 'cylinder lawn mower', 'chilled cast-iron', 'traction engine' and many hundreds more.

The Industrial Revolution in England gathered momentum throughout the eighteenth century and reached a peak in Victorian times. The overall effect would change the English way of life more

dramatically than perhaps any other event in history. Mechanisation in the agricultural industry required a smaller labour force, which in turn gave other industries a valuable manpower resource. This would enable them to improve production to meet the ever-increasing demand for goods from the growing population.

Advances made in mechanisation, new inventions and a different attitude towards natural resources meant that the whole infrastructure of England would change. A mass migration from the countryside to the towns in search of employment occurred, and urban-industrial life on a scale never seen before would emerge. Big commercial business enterprises dominated large parts of the landscape, especially in the Midlands and the north of England. Coal mining increased at an extraordinary rate, with new machinery going further down into the ground replacing open-cast mining near the surface.

Harnessing of steam power along with the improvements in iron and steel production meant that practically every industry would be affected. The manufacture of textiles would move from the cottage industry it once was to labour-intensive factories. Yorkshire became the centre for the wool trade and Lancashire the cotton industry.

The chemical industry grew with the increased demand for sodium carbonate in the glass, soap and paper industries. There was greater need for sulphuric acid in iron and steel foundries and for bleaching cloth in the textile industry. Cement was invented for use in the construction of canals, roadways, buildings, tunnels, and so on. The advances in gas lighting not only benefited domestic households, but meant that factories could stay open longer and increase production. The manufacture of glass was revolutionised with plate and sheet glass being available for the first time. The continuous production method of making paper made the printing and publication of books, pamphlets, magazines, periodicals, and eventually newspapers, cheaper. Many other industries were affected and would never be the same again.

Perhaps some of the biggest strides would be in transport. The use of waterways, the building of canals and eventually the building of the railways, especially the latter, would see England edge out front as a world leader. Rail links would eventually cross vast areas of the Empire, and they were laid by British engineers using equipment, machinery and engines made in England.

The invention of the telegraph changed communications worldwide. From humble beginnings, the telegraph network tended to follow the same routes as the railway lines, connecting distant towns and cities with virtually instant communications. More inventions and modifications, along with advances in submarine cable laying, allowed the telegraph system to reach across the Atlantic to the USA and Canada. Australia was linked to London in the late Victorian era – for the first time all parts of the Empire were connected.

Whilst this industrial expansion may have been beneficial to the wealth of the nation, landowners, industrialists, capitalists and the like, it certainly would have an adverse effect on the many millions of ordinary working folk in the factories and the mines. Industrialisation would scar large swathes of the landscape, and pollution would become a problem with untreated industrial and chemical waste. The boom in population had created the added problem of sewage disposal – or more accurately the lack of sewage disposal. Existence was hard in these industrial areas, with low rates of life expectancy, high infant mortality rates, child labour prevalent in all industries (including working down the mines), harsh conditions for women, squalid housing conditions and chronic hunger and malnutrition all becoming the norm.

Industrial unrest reared its head with riots, the most famous being the Luddite Riots in the early 1800s in the North West. These were named after a worker called Ned Ludd, who had infamously sabotaged a machine that he saw as replacing his job and the jobs of other skilled workers. The Luddites, through fear of unemployment, made a series of raids destroying machinery that could be operated by less skilled workers on lower pay. The general unrest in the North West was made worse with the periods of famine and a rise in unemployment after the Napoleonic Wars. The people of Manchester and its surrounding areas wanted to have some form of political reform and to be given some influence to try and improve their harsh living conditions. A large crowd of around 70,000 people gathered at St Peter's Field in Manchester to peacefully demonstrate against their plight and make their demands publicly known. The magistrates called for the military to disperse the crowd with no instructions as to how. The military carried out their orders with a cavalry charge into the crowd, wielding their sabres. Fifteen people were killed and several hundred were injured. It became known as the Peterloo Massacre.

'Luddite' has entered the English language as a generic term for someone who fears the advent of new technology and destroys or holds up production. Luddism has become synonymous with attitudes of resistance against changes in technology and production methods. 'Peterloo' was a composite of St Peter's Field, where the demonstration took place, plus 'Waterloo' after the famous battle against Napoleon;

Some words and phrases that entered the English language from advances in agriculture, industry, science and medicine 1700AD to 1900AD

acne	agoraphobia	ambulance	aniline
bacteria	benzene	biology	blowing cylinders
caffeine	carding machines	centigrade	chloroform
chromosome	chronometer	claustrophobia	combine harvester
combustion engine	condenser	cotton gin	cotton mill
cylinder boring machine	Davy lamp	diphtheria	donkey engine
electric motor	electron	entomology	ethnology
flying shuttle	foundry cupola	gas lamp	gas light
gynaecology	halogen	histology	hot blast
hydraulic power	hypochondria	hypothalamus	hysteria
lawnmower	lens	lithograph	Luddite
machine tools	macintosh	morphology	oxygen
palaeontology	pasteurise	Peterloo Massacre	petrology
piston	power loom	protein	psychiatry
psychosis	rail locomotive	railway	railway lines
refraction	reservoir	reverberatory furnace	roller spinning frame
rolling mill	safety lamp	spinning mule	spinning jenny
steam boats	steam engines	steam locomotive	steam power
steam pulley	steam train	stethoscope	streptococcus
tarmacadam	taxonomy	telephone	telegraph
telegraph poles	telegraph wires	typist	typewriter
vaccination	vaccine	vacuum flask	vacuum pump

Fig 50

233

the actions of the military at St Peter's Field were likened to that of a cavalry charge in battle.

A few words and phrases deriving from the hardships of the working classes and unemployed became part of the common English vocabulary, including new concepts such as the 'trade union' and 'strike action'. The vast majority of new words came from advances and discoveries made in science, medicine, exploration and technology. Progress in these areas meant that thousands of words and phrases would enter the English vocabulary and numerous combinations of words would take on other meanings. Much of the new vocabulary in science-based subjects and medical terminology was formed using Latin and Greek as the basis, as in centigrade from the Latin for 100 (*centum*) and steps (*gradus*); the 'lens' of a telescope is from the Latin *lens* for being shaped like a lentil. Examples of Greek words include 'electron' from *elektron,* which means amber, from which the Ancient Greeks supposedly generated some form of energy, whilst 'hydraulics' derives from *hudraulikos,* meaning water (*hudro*) pipe (*aulos*). New branches of science and medicine were created and developed during this period, many with Greek-based suffixes of -*logy* or -*ology* (study of a particular subject), -*nomy* or -*onomy* (a system of rules) and -*graphy* or -*ography* (writing). Examples of these suffixes being used to make up words for new industrial, scientific and medical developments are 'ethnology' (study of different peoples), 'entomology' (study of insects), 'petrology' (study of rocks), 'taxonomy' (rules on classification) and 'photography' (writing with light).

England led the world in industrialisation and advances in medical and scientific research throughout the Georgian period and into Victoria's reign. However, in the middle-to-late nineteenth century England was overtaken by the USA as the industrial world leader. The rise of America as an industrial nation and eventual world power would have an effect on the English language, not only in America but also in England. The latter is decribed in the chapter 'The American Influence' (page 238).

Education in Georgian times and the Victorian era would have a marked influence on the English language. Initially it would highlight the difference in society between the wealthier classes and the poor. The standards in the English language that were evolving, both in grammar and pronunciation, were being promoted and taught in the education system at the time, which favoured greatly those who could pay the school fees. This created a greater divide between the well-educated rich minority speaking a standardised English and the poorer uneducated majority maintaining their regional dialects. However, this situation would gradually start to change as education became more readily accessible to the working classes and the poor.

During the time of the Stuarts, the Society for Promoting Christian Knowledge went from strength to strength and founded many charity schools for the children of the poor aged between seven and eleven years, and became the forerunner for a more widespread primary and secondary education in the next century. It was also unique in that the society carried out teacher training, as well, albeit at a fairly basic level.

The Sunday School Movement, initiated by Robert Raikes, had a great success in providing education to the less fortunate from the late 1700s onwards. At first, these boys-only schools were open only on a Sunday because the boys would invariably be working the other six days of the week. The boys were taught to read from the Bible and then proceeded to learn the Catechism. School would be from 10 a.m. to noon, after which the boys would go home for lunch and return for 1 p.m. They would continue their education until it was time to be accompanied to church. After church the boys would return to school until 5 p.m. and then were ordered home with strict instructions to remain silent and be respectful of the Sabbath. Girls were allowed to attend once the schools had become established, but by the end of the 1700s the Sunday School Movement was under threat and many closed. This was due to the fierce opposition from devout Christians who thought that the Sabbath was a day of rest and that paying teachers to work on that day went against Christian principles. Despite this blip, Sunday Schools throughout Great Britain were providing an education to approximately a quarter of all seven- to eleven-year-olds in the early 1800s.

In 1811 National Schools were founded by the National Society for Promoting the Education of the Poor in the Principles of the Established Church in England and Wales. They became very popular and some are still in existence today as voluntary-aided or controlled schools, although state-funded.

The year 1833 was a milestone in state education. For the first time in history, Parliament agreed to allocate money annually for the building of schools for the children of the poor. Seven years later the Grammar School Act stated that science and English literature should be part of a national curriculum.

Progress in state education for all children continued slowly until the Elementary Education Act of 1870, which stated that partially

state-funded schools were to be established to provide primary education in areas that had an unsatisfactory system. Schools were to continue to be fee-paying but the very poor were exempt; attendance was compulsory with few exceptions. Ten years later another Elementary Education Act endorsed the previous one with a few amendments, and in 1893 the school leaving age was raised to eleven. The Act was amended in the same year to include special provision for blind and deaf children, who up until that point had never received any official or formal education – a milestone in the provision of education that is often overlooked. In 1889 the school leaving age was changed again and raised to twelve.

The overall influence on spoken English due to the increase in education for all children, regardless of social standing, would have a lasting effect. It would be gradual but the first steps had been taken to close the divide between the well educated, wealthier members of society speaking Standard English and the less educated, poorer classes speaking in strong dialects. Children in all schools would be taught to read from books written in Standard English, and likewise in their lessons on English grammar.

Eventually, over a very long period of time, well into the twentieth century and perhaps beyond, English dialects would become diluted and continue just as accents. Children were now learning Standard English words and grammar that tended to replace the vocabulary and grammatical structure of any particular dialect. There was, however, now an increasing tendency for formal elocution to be taught in the rich public and private fee-paying schools, whilst the pronunciation of a dialect, its accent, was left untouched in other schools. The gap had started to narrow, but would it ever close?

14

The American Influence

By the end of the eighteenth century Johnson's dictionaries, Murray's book on English grammar and Sheridan's publication on pronunciation were spectacularly popular, both in England and America. They were also used extensively in the education system of both countries. As previously mentioned, it is reasonable to assume, therefore, that the standards of English in both were more alike in pronunciation, grammar and spelling than at any time before or since. Thereafter the English language would develop differently in both countries.

It has been said that Standard English was 'written by gentlemen, for gentlemen, to distinguish them from the laborious working classes'. This notion was fully endorsed in the late 1700s when Noah Webster, an American educationalist and grammarian, stated that the English language had been corrupted by the British aristocracy, which had set its own standards for proper spelling and pronunciation. This observation was very true in the late 1700s, when *The Times* newspaper was first published in England along with very prestigious and fashionable periodicals such as *Tatler* and *The Spectator*. These publications would become very popular amongst the more elite members of society in England, and between them endorsed the standards of English at the time and greatly influenced its style.

Webster objected to American children being taught English with textbooks from England. He believed that they should be taught with American books – so much so that he wrote *A Grammatical Institute of the English Language* to be used in American schools. This was made up of three volumes, separately published between 1783 and 1785. It eventually became very popular, with many editions printed during the next fifty years. Webster wanted to save the American way of speaking from being influenced by the 'clamour of pedantry' and dogmatism of Standard English with its elitist, anti-democratic associations. He was also of the belief that the study of Latin and Greek should not be mandatory before studying English; he believed that grammar should be based on common acceptance and usage rather than the prescriptions of ancient languages.

Webster's greatest works were his dictionaries. The first, in 1806, entitled *A Compendious Dictionary of the English Language*, was followed twenty-seven years later, after extensive research, with his *An American Dictionary of the English Language*. He had learned nearly thirty languages to verify origins of English words, but controversially preferred spellings to match pronunciation, as in *theater* and *humor*. Webster also entered words adopted from Native Americans, such as *wigwam* and *tomahawk*.

Webster's dictionary contained nearly 70,000 words, which included approximately 12,000 words previously unrecorded in any dictionary. When published it received many bad reviews, especially from traditionalists who condemned it as breaking away from true English. These condemnations reflected the standards of American English at the turn of the eighteenth century being not too dissimilar to that of Standard English. Eventually, after his death, Webster's dictionary was replaced with an abbreviated version omitting the controversial spellings. It became a bestseller.

It would appear that during the nineteenth and twentieth centuries Standard English would be the one to change more radically than American English, and it is very reasonable to assume that the latter is much nearer in pronunciation to Early Modern English than is Standard English. The Americans have held on to a number of Elizabethan words, such as *gotten,* which have disappeared from use in England. However, many of these old words have been reintroduced into the English vocabulary, such as 'bug' and 'cabin' and many more.

Americans also created new words and phrases. This was evident in their literature, which became popular in England during the latter half of the nineteenth century, and included such works as *Uncle Tom's Cabin* and *Huckleberry Finn*. As a result, many new Americanisms entered the English vocabulary such as 'skedaddle', 'riff-raff', 'hunky-dory', 'bamboozle' and 'humdinger'. American phrases and idioms would become popular, such as 'knuckle down', 'bite the dust', 'barking up the wrong tree', 'fly off the handle' and

'strike it rich'. It is also believed that because the Americans saw the English speaking with their strict Standard English enunciation that necessitated an immobile upper lip to pronounce it, no matter what the circumstances, the phrase 'stiff upper lip' possibly came about.

Through time, American literature became more popular in England, as did films with the advent of the movies and Hollywood, along with songs, music and dance and many American programmes on television. The Americans fought as allies in two world wars and still maintain British-based airfields. All these factors, together with the age of the computer, mean that even more Americanisms and phrases have been adopted into the English vocabulary. Examples of these phrases include 'no axe to grind', 'sitting on the fence', 'poker face', 'stake a claim', and words such as 'bedrock', 'smooch', 'raincoat', 'skyscraper', 'joyride', 'showdown', 'cocktail', 'cookie' and many more.

The enduring American influence on modern English should not be underestimated.

15

The Twentieth Century to the Modern Day

Modern life would change dramatically throughout the twentieth century and the beginning of the twenty-first. Ordinary travel would go from being undertaken mainly by horses and carts and occasional rail journeys to nearly every family owning a motor car. Dual carriageways and the introduction of motorways responded to the increase in road traffic, changing the landscape forever. Travel by air would become normal practice, and outer-space exploration would see a man landing on the moon and unmanned craft venturing off to other planets.

There would be the misery, turmoil and aftermath of two lengthy, catastrophic world wars, with many millions of lives lost and many more being permanently damaged and scarred. Large numbers of the population struggled to survive living in and around old bomb sites. During the slum clearance programmes many communities were re-housed a considerable distance away from their homes in new towns and housing estates being built in various parts of the country.

The advent of radio and television would reach the vast majority of homes nationwide and create new domestic customs and habits centred around 'the box'. There was a cultural revolution in the late 1950s and 1960s that permanently changed attitudes, music, fashions and many aspects of previously held social norms. Many people from countries in the Commonwealth, formerly the British Empire, started to arrive in Britain in great numbers, as did people from the European Union and further afield.

The telephone was originally a luxury item for the wealthier classes that eventually became a common household item. The arrival of the mobile phone would radically change communications for nearly everyone in all walks of life. The age of the computer would revolutionise nearly every facet of society, commerce and industry. Standards of living rose for the vast majority of the country, and more young people attended further education after the building of many new colleges and universities.

The English language would be greatly affected by all these events and the English vocabulary would absorb thousands of new words and phrases. Some would be existing words with new meanings, such as 'mouse' in computer terminology. Others would be new innovations, such as 'bumf' for useless printed material, originating from 'bum fodder', First World War soldier slang for toilet paper. Many new words would be adopted from people entering from overseas such as the different styles of Caribbean music, 'calypso', 'ska' and 'reggae'.

The first major event in this period was the First World War from 1914 to 1918, with many British troops fighting on the Western Front in atrocious conditions. Many sailors were members of ships' crews either taking part in momentous sea conflicts such as the Battle of Jutland or more commonly were part of the merchant fleet delivering essential food supplies. The RFC and then RAF was founded and pilots took to the air to defend the homeland. The entire war effort at home, abroad and at sea would create a whole new vocabulary that would be adopted into general use, sometimes only briefly, but very often on a more permanent basis. Words like 'sniper', 'snapshot', 'trench coat', 'conked out', 'camouflage', 'blind spot', 'duckboard', 'shell shock', 'snuffed it' and many more. 'Dear Old Blighty' became a common phrase used by British troops longing for home, and was an adaptation of *bilayati,* coined from and made popular by the Indian troops on the front line.

The First World War also showed the vast differences between the various strata of English society, as was highlighted in the *Wipers Times*, a wartime spoof newspaper published in the trenches to boost the morale of troops on the front at Ypres. It was towards the end of the war, in 1917, when the snobbery surrounding a particular type of spoken English was endorsed. Daniel Jones, a phonetician and Head of Phonetics at University College London, initiated the idea of Public School Pronunciation (PSP) in a book entitled *English Pronouncing Dictionary*. He described the existence of an offshoot of Standard English as spoken by the well-educated middle and upper classes whose menfolk had attended Cambridge and Oxford universities, having been previously educated at schools like Harrow, Eton, Westminster and Winchester. He described them as the 'great public boarding schools'. Influential professions such as law, accountancy, politics, and the clergy engaged many from this privileged background with their PSP accents. Jones's book excluded dictionary definitions and avoided English grammar. The book was strictly focussed on pronunciation, based solely on the PSP used in those public schools and universities previously mentioned; there was to be no hint whatsoever of any regional dialect. The *English Pronouncing Dictionary* proved to be very popular especially in London and the south-east of England, so much so that it was adopted in principle by the BBC.

In the 1920s the BBC launched its national radio service and a small committee, which included Daniel Jones, was formed to establish the correct English pronunciation to use in broadcasting. PSP, which by this time was being referred to as Received Pronunciation (RP), was the basis for the BBC English accent. In 1928 the committee produced a list of recommendations entitled *Broadcast English*, followed by a revised edition three years later. The standards they had set for BBC English were to stay with the Corporation, with a few minor adjustments, for many years, including the early days of television.

Members of the Royal Family benefited from a privileged public school education and private tutoring, and the lessons they had received influenced the way they spoke, resulting in the RP accent. Consequently RP, or BBC English, was regularly referred to as 'King's English' or 'Queen's English' and often mistakenly referred to as Standard English. Many prime ministers and eminent politicians, such as Sir Winston Churchill, had also received a privileged education and spoke with an RP accent.

The BBC was being listened to by millions of people throughout the land and overseas. Some of the special programmes would include royal Christmas messages and the king's wartime speeches, and interviews with prime ministers and eminent politicians would be broadcast – all with the RP of the BBC English accent. The differences between the BBC accent and the regional dialects of most of the listeners were therefore highlighted. An elitist social cachet surrounded RP, with provincial accents, seldom broadcast, being very much frowned upon and dismissed. The sizeable adverse reaction in the 1940s to the BBC diverting away from their norm and employing a newsreader with a Yorkshire dialect was immense. The furore emphasised the snobbery associated with the BBC accent and they quickly returned to BBC English.

However, it would be the BBC itself that eventually broke down the snobbery surrounding this posh accent. In the second half of the twentieth century the BBC introduced regional news programmes on television and eventually launched around forty local radio stations. Many presenters on both radio and TV would have distinct regional dialects, including famous sports commentators like Peter O'Sullevan (Irish) and Bill McClaren (Scottish).

Right from the start, words, terms and phrases used during broadcasting would enter the English vocabulary, such as 'radio', 'back to square one', 'going for an early bath', 'on the box' and many more.

During the early twentieth century another big step was taken in the history of the English language. In 1928 the *Oxford English Dictionary* was first published as one complete work, in twelve volumes and with 415,000 entries, which represented the culmination of nearly seventy years' research and compiling. In 1857 the Philological Society of London felt that the dictionaries of the time were wholly inadequate and incomplete, and they wanted a complete overhaul of English, right from its very beginnings in Anglo-Saxon times. After much deliberation, a contract was finalised two years later with the Oxford University Press to compile a *New English Dictionary on Historical Principles*. Thereafter a great deal of research was meticulously conducted and, finally, in 1884, the first fascicle A to B Volume 1 was printed. Another 124 fascicles would be published in the next four decades, and in 1928 the complete works were published as the *Oxford English Dictionary* (otherwise known as the OED). It was soon realised once completed that many entries were out of date because the English language was constantly readjusting and changing with the times, and continues to do so.

After two further supplements, a complete second edition was published in 1989, some 100 years after the first fascicle. This time, however, it was in twenty volumes and recorded more than 615,000 entries. Each entry has a history including its original spelling, how and when it was first recorded, with its definition and a usage illustrated in quotations and examples. It also shows how each word is pronounced and because of the OED's reputation and standing, it is recognised as the unofficial authority and standard for the pronunciation of words in the English language and the basis for a recognised standard in modern use.

Computer technology in the industrial and commercial world, electronics, the media, communications, travel, leisure and the home,

have all had an immeasurable affect on nearly every facet of everyday life. They have also had a big input into the English language, with hundreds of new words entering the vocabulary. Words such as 'software', 'megabytes', 'cyberspace', 'laptop', 'microchip', 'hacker', 'internet' and many more have been adopted and become part of common use. Some nouns have also been turned into verbs, such as (to) 'Google' and (to) 'text', as in 'I will google it,' and 'I texted her yesterday'. Texting has also popularised an abbreviated language, especially amongst the younger members of society, with examples such as *lol, ttfn, cul8ter, plz* and a great many more, some unsuitable for those who have had a sheltered upbringing.

16

Conclusion

The English language has progressed from very humble beginnings as a Germanic dialect of invading settlers in Britain in the fifth century to a global language in the twenty-first century. It is a rich language with tens of thousands more words in its vocabulary than any other language.

English has never been officially standardised by a royal decree, government department or any other official body. It has evolved through the centuries despite there being many attempts by grammarians, lexicographers, linguists and phoneticians to try and create a once-and-for-all standard. This goal was never achievable. As English developed over the ages it adopted many thousands of words through overseas exploration, international trade and from building a global empire. Technical advances and new terminology during the Agricultural and Industrial Revolutions and afterwards, including the age of the computer, have constantly brought new words into the language. During the Renaissance period many thousands of words were created and entered into the English vocabulary along with adopted words from Italy. Changes in culture from medieval times to the present day have created new expressions and ways of saying things. The continual changes throughout the ages in entertainment, communications and latterly the media, are also accountable for thousands of new words and terminology becoming part of everyday usage. Through the years, the various translations of the Bible into English have had a lasting effect and provided the source of innumerable English phrases, idioms and proverbs and provided the basis of a Standard English. The education system from Alfred the Great's time to the 1800s and early 1900s highlighted the divide between the educated and uneducated, and during the nineteenth century culminated in the creation of a class-bound English accent. However, free state education also had a levelling effect on the English language.

With all these continuing changes in society throughout history, the English language was never able to stay still. It has continually responded to and kept abreast of the times. Therefore, the many learned men who tried to analyse the language and create a standard were fighting a losing battle, especially when they could not agree amongst themselves. Some were very proscriptive as to how English grammar, spelling and pronunciation ought to be, and took little notice of the dialects of the general public. Other grammarians thought that a standard ought to be based descriptively on common usage.

As a result, regional dialects have held their ground and English has never been officially formalised. It has remained untamed with many variations and exceptions to the norm. This has led to words that can be spelled the same and mean the same thing but have different pronunciations, such as 'garage' and 'controversy'. English also has words that can be spelled the same but have different pronunciations and meanings, such as 'invalid' and 'minute'. It has also resulted in English having many more different words having the same meaning than any other language.

Its development has culminated in a language that is both ancient and modern, with a very rich vocabulary that moves with the times. It has meant that English literature has a vast and nuanced lexicon that has the ability to express itself in many wonderful and dramatic ways, and has been universally recognised and travelled the world. Chaucer, Shakespeare, Dickens, Agatha Christie, Conan Doyle – Enid Blyton – English authors, playwrights and poets have been translated into many different languages.

Where languages have been rigidly standardised and maintained they have died, such as Latin and Ancient Greek. It is arguably true that French will see the same demise with an Ancient or Academic French, as preserved by the Académie Francaise, becoming a thing of the past, and a Modern French, reflecting the way the French people have continued to express themselves, becoming the unofficial standard.

English does not have that problem because it continues to respond and adjust to modern advances and keeps abreast of changes in society. It is these qualities in the English language that make it the richest

Some examples of words spelled the same with:-
a. Different pronunciations but same meanings

alternative pronunciations	alternative pronunciations	alternative pronunciations
abseil • abzil or absail	absorb • abzorb or ab-sorb	actual • act-ual or ac-chooal
almond • arm'nd or al-m'nd	amen • armen or aymen	ate • ayt or ett
auction • orksh'n or oksh'n	conduit • con-juit or con-duit	conch • kongk or konch
concord • konkord or kong-kord	either • eether or eye-the	eyot • eye-ot or ait
giraffe • jiraff or jerarf	harass • ha-r'ss or her-rass	harem • har-reem or hair-r'm
hotel • o-tell or ho-tel	hurricane • hurryk'n or kane	italics • eye-tallics or it-allics
lichen • liken or litchen	migraine • mygrain or megrain	neither • neether or nye-the
off • orff or off	omit • omm-it or o-mit	patent • pat-ent or payt'nt
patriot • pat or payt-re-ut	poet • po-it or po-et	procure • pro or pra-cure
proceed • pro or pra-seed	schedule • sked or shed-ule	urine • you-rine or you-rin
visual • viz-ual or vijj-ual	valet • vall-et or vallay	vitamin • vite or vit-a-m'n

b. Different pronunciations and different meanings

alternative pronunciations	alternative pronunciations	alternative pronunciations
alternate • olta-nate or oltern-ut	bow • rhymes with cow or toe	compact • compact or c'mpact
conduct • conduct or c'nduct	conflict • conflict or c'nflict	consort • consort or c'nsort
correct • cor-rect or c'rrect	desert • dezut or deezert	divers • di v'z or di verz
graduate • gradu-ut or gradu-ate	have • hav or haff	invalid • in-val-id or inverlid
live • liv or rhymes with hive	minute • minnit or my-nute	polish • pollish or Po-lish
present • pree-zent or prez'nt	produce • prer or prod-uce	rebel • reebell or rebble
record • reck-ord or ree-cord	refuse • reefuze or reffuce	resume • rezoom or rez-u-may
row • rhymes with cow or toe	sewer • sue-er or so-er	sow • rhymes with cow or toe
use • youss or yooze	wind • winned or wined	wound • woond or wown'd

Fig 51

language in the world. It will continue to be so if future grammarians, lexicographers and phoneticians simply record the development and evolution of the English language, rather than prescribing how it should be written or pronounced.

English dialects are an integral part of the language and should never be discouraged. They are rich with linguistic traditions and replete with history, with many ancient words and phrases deriving from Anglo-Saxon and Old Norse origins – much more so than Standard English. They are part of our heritage.

Despite all its empire building, industrial and commercial advancements and discoveries in technology, the greatest gift England has given to the world is surely the English language.

Select Bibliography

Ackroyd, P., *The History of England: Volume 1 Foundation* (London: Macmillan, 2011)

Auden, W. H., *An Elizabethan Song Book* (London: Faber and Faber, 1957)

Bragg, M., *The Adventure of English: 500AD to 2000 The Biography of a Language* (London: Hodder & Stoughton, 2003)

Brook, G. L., *English Sound-Changes* (Manchester: Manchester University Press, 1957)

Clark Hall, J. R., *A Concise Anglo-Saxon Dictionary* (Cambridge: Cambridge University Press, 1960)

Crossley-Holland, K., *The Poetry of Legend: Classics of the Medieval World: Beowulf* (Woodbridge: Boydell & Brewer, 1987)

Crystal, D. and Crystal, B., *Oxford Illustrated Shakespeare Dictionary* (Oxford: Oxford University Press, 2015)

Crystal, D., *The Stories of English* (London: Penguin Books, 2005)

Dunton-Downer, L. and Riding, A., *Essential Shakespeare Handbook* (London: Dorling Kindersley, 2004)

Flavell, L. and Flavell, R., (Leicester: Silverdale Books, 1999)

Forby, Rev. R., *The Vocabulary of East Anglia* (London: J. B. Nichols, 1830)

Guy, J., *Drake and the Elizabethan Explorers* (Tonbridge: Ticktock Publishing, 1998)

Halliday, F. E., *Doctor Johnson and his World* (London: Thames and Hudson, 1968)

Heaney, S., *Beowulf* (London: Faber and Faber, 1999)

Hynde, T., *The Domesday Book: England's Heritage, Then and Now* (Frome: Book Club Associates, 1985)

Jenkins, S., *A Short History of England* (London: Profile Books, 2011)

Jonson, B., *English Grammar* (Milton Keynes: Lightning Source UK Ltd., 2015)

Leach, A., *The Letter H, Past, Present, and Future* (London: Griffith & Farran, 1880)

McArthur, T., *The Oxford Companion to the English Language* (Oxford: Oxford University Press, 1992)

McCrum, R., Cran, W., MacNeil, R., *The Story of English* (London: Faber and Faber, 1986)

Miles, D., *The Tribes of Britain* (London: Phoenix, 2006)

Mills, A. D., A Dictionary of British Place Names (Oxford: Oxford University Press, 2011)

Mills, A. D., A Dictionary of London Place-Names (Oxford: Oxford University Press, 2004)

Nicolson, A., *When God Spoke English: The Making Of the King James Bible* (London: Harper Press, 2004)

Quennell, P., *A History of English Literature* (London: Weidenfeld and Nicholson, 1973)

Reaney, P. H., *A Dictionary of English Surnames* (Oxford: Oxford University Press, 1997)

Reaney, P. H., *The Origin of English Surnames* (London: Routledge & Keegan Paul, 1967)

Rogers, P., *The Oxford Illustrated History of English Literature* (Oxford: Oxford University Press, 1987)

Scholes, P. A., *The Oxford Companion to Music* (Oxford: Oxford University Press, 1996)

Strong, R., *The Story of Britain* (London: Hutchinson, 1996)

Williams, N., *Francis Drake* (London: Weidenfeld and Nicholson, 1973)

Woods, W., *England in the Age of Chaucer* (London: Hart-Davis, MacGibbon, 1976)

The Holy Bible: Authorised King James Version

The Book of Common Prayer